OFFICERS

Boris Shishkin, *Chairman*
Harry Scherman, *President*
C. C. Balderston, *Vice-President*
George B. Roberts, *Treasurer*
W. J. Carson, *Executive Director*
Martha Anderson, *Editor*

DIRECTORS AT LARGE

D. R. Belcher, *American Telephone & Telegraph Co.*
Oswald W. Knauth, *Beaufort, South Carolina*
Simon Kuznets, *University of Pennsylvania*
H. W. Laidler, *Executive Director, League for Industrial Democracy*
Shepard Morgan, *New York City*
C. Reinold Noyes, *Princeton, New Jersey*
George B. Roberts, *Vice-President, National City Bank*
Beardsley Ruml, *New York City*
Harry Scherman, *Chairman, Book-of-the-Month Club*
George Soule, *Bennington College*
N. I. Stone, *Consulting Economist*
J. Raymond Walsh, *WMCA Broadcasting Co.*
Leo Wolman, *Columbia University*
Theodore O. Yntema, *Vice President-Finance, Ford Motor Company*

DIRECTORS BY UNIVERSITY APPOINTMENT

E. Wight Bakke, *Yale*	H. M. Groves, *Wisconsin*
C. C. Balderston, *Pennsylvania*	Gottfried Haberler, *Harvard*
Arthur F. Burns, *Columbia*	Clarence Heer, *North Carolina*
G. A. Elliott, *Toronto*	R. L. Kozelka, *Minnesota*
Frank W. Fetter, *Northwestern*	Paul M. O'Leary, *Cornell*

T. W. Schultz, *Chicago*

DIRECTORS APPOINTED BY OTHER ORGANIZATIONS

Percival F. Brundage, *American Institute of Accountants*
Thomas C. Cochran, *Economic History Association*
Frederick C. Mills, *American Statistical Association*
S. H. Ruttenberg, *Congress of Industrial Organizations*
Murray Shields, *American Management Association*
Boris Shishkin, *American Federation of Labor*
Donald H. Wallace, *American Economic Association*
Frederick V. Waugh, *American Farm Economic Association*

RESEARCH STAFF

Arthur F. Burns, *Director of Research*
Geoffrey H. Moore, *Associate Director of Research*

Moses Abramovitz	F. F. Hill
Harold Barger	Thor Hultgren
Morris A. Copeland	Simon Kuznets
Daniel Creamer	Clarence D. Long
David Durand	Ruth P. Mack
Solomon Fabricant	Frederick C. Mills
Milton Friedman	Raymond J. Saulnier
Millard Hastay	Lawrence H. Seltzer
W. Braddock Hickman	George J. Stigler

Leo Wolman

Relation of the Directors to the Work and Publications of the National Bureau of Economic Research

1. The object of the National Bureau of Economic Research is to ascertain and to present to the public important economic facts and their interpretation in a scientific and impartial manner. The Board of Directors is charged with the responsibility of ensuring that the work of the National Bureau is carried on in strict conformity with this object.

2. To this end the Board of Directors shall appoint one or more Directors of Research.

3. The Director or Directors of Research shall submit to the members of the Board, or to its Executive Committee, for their formal adoption, all specific proposals concerning researches to be instituted.

4. No report shall be published until the Director or Directors of Research shall have submitted to the Board a summary drawing attention to the character of the data and their utilization in the report, the nature and treatment of the problems involved, the main conclusions and such other information as in their opinion would serve to determine the suitability of the report for publication in accordance with the principles of the National Bureau.

5. A copy of any manuscript proposed for publication shall also be submitted to each member of the Board. For each manuscript to be so submitted a special committee shall be appointed by the President, or at his designation by the Executive Director, consisting of three Directors selected as nearly as may be one from each general division of the Board. The names of the special manuscript committee shall be stated to each Director when the summary and report described in paragraph (4) are sent to him. It shall be the duty of each member of the committee to read the manuscript. If each member of the special committee signifies his approval within thirty days, the manuscript may be published. If each member of the special committee has not signified his approval within thirty days of the transmittal of the report and manuscript, the Director of Research shall then notify each member of the Board, requesting approval or disapproval of publication, and thirty additional days shall be granted for this purpose. The manuscript shall then not be published unless at least a majority of the entire Board and a two-thirds majority of those members of the Board who shall have voted on the proposal within the time fixed for the receipt of votes on the publication proposed shall have approved.

6. No manuscript may be published, though approved by each member of the special committee, until forty-five days have elapsed from the transmittal of the summary and report. The interval is allowed for the receipt of any memorandum of dissent or reservation, together with a brief statement of his reasons, that any member may wish to express; and such memorandum of dissent or reservation shall be published with the manuscript if he so desires. Publication does not, however, imply that each member of the Board has read the manuscript, or that either members of the Board in general, or of the special committee, have passed upon its validity in every detail.

7. A copy of this resolution shall, unless otherwise determined by the Board, be printed in each copy of every National Bureau book.

(Resolution adopted October 25, 1926 and revised February 6, 1933 and February 24, 1941)

PUBLICATIONS OF THE
NATIONAL BUREAU OF ECONOMIC RESEARCH, INC.
NUMBER 52

DETERIORATION IN THE QUALITY

OF FOREIGN BONDS ISSUED

IN THE UNITED STATES

1920-1930

Deterioration in the Quality of Foreign Bonds Issued in the United States 1920-1930

by Ilse Mintz
Columbia University

National Bureau of
Economic Research, Inc.

Copyright, 1951, by

National Bureau of Economic Research, Inc.

1819 Broadway, New York 23

All Rights Reserved

Composition by Oscar Leventhal, Inc.

Presswork and binding by H. Wolff

Author's Acknowledgements

My biggest debt is due Arthur F. Burns from whose unfailing encouragement and valuable advice I benefited immensely throughout my work. Special thanks go to Geoffrey H. Moore who contributed greatly to the substance and form of the study. Ragnar Nurkse's comments were especially helpful and highly appreciated. I am grateful for useful suggestions by Frederick C. Mills, Solomon Fabricant, and W. Braddock Hickman of the Research Staff; by G. A. Elliott, Frank W. Fetter, and Shepard Morgan, Directors of the National Bureau; and by Antonin Basch and J. Lynch of the International Bank.

I am obliged to Millard Hastay and the members of the Business Cycle unit for their help with the statistical analysis, to H. Irving Forman for his competent execution of the charts, and to Hanna Stern for making the index.

A grant from the Social Science Research Council which enabled me to do much of the research connected with this study is acknowledged with gratitude.

Contents

Introduction ... 1
  1 Current Opinions on Foreign Lending ... 1
  2 Nature of the Study ... 3
  3 Some Remarks on Our Findings ... 6

CHAPTER

1 The Volume of Foreign Lending ... 8
  1 Scope of the Investigation ... 8
  2 Cycles in Foreign Lending ... 11
  3 The Balance of Payments and Foreign Bond Cycles ... 13
  4 Foreign Business Cycles and Bond Cycles ... 15
    a) Cycles in Debtor Countries ... 15
    b) Cycles in Foreign Creditor Countries ... 18
  5 American Business Cycles and Foreign Bond Cycles ... 20
    a) Cycles in Domestic Bond Issues ... 20
    b) Common Stock Issues and Foreign Bond Cycles ... 24

2 The Default Index ... 29
  1 The Sound Loan Curve ... 31
  2 Definition of the Default Index ... 32
  3 Description of the Default Index ... 37
  4 Degree of Default ... 40
  5 Note on the Present Status of Foreign Bonds ... 43
  6 In Conclusion ... 45
  7 Note on Two Investigations of Investment Quality ... 45

3 Geographic Shifts in Foreign Loans ... 50

4 Quality of Foreign Loans Initiated by Individual Banking Houses ... 54

5 The Risk Premium ... 59

6 An Interpretation ... 63
  1 The Picture of Change ... 63
  2 Analysis of Change ... 68
  3 Role of the Banking Houses ... 72
    a) Banking Estimates of Risk ... 73
    b) The Importance of Risk ... 78
  4 The Demand of the Public ... 80
    a) Who is 'The Public'? ... 80
    b) Why Does the Public Buy Foreign Bonds? ... 81
    c) How Did the Change in the Public's Attitude Affect the Bankers? ... 82

TABLE

1	Total Foreign Dollar Capital Issues, Governmental and Private, Publicly Offered in the United States	9
2	Foreign Government Bonds Issued in the United States Compared with Business Cycles in the Borrowing Country and in the United States, 1920-1930	17
3	Foreign Government Securities Issued in the United Kingdom and in the United States, 1920-1930	19
4	Conformity to Business Cycles, Foreign Government and Domestic Bonds Issued in the United States	22
5	Foreign Common Stock and Foreign Government Bonds Issued in the United States	28
6	Default Status of Domestic Bonds Outstanding in December 1931, by Date of Issue	46
7	Foreclosure rates on a Sample of Urban Mortgage Loans Made by Life Insurance Companies	48
8	Annual Default Index: Argentina, Cuba, Panama	51
9	Default Index, 5 Geographic Areas	51
10	Distribution by Geographic Areas, Foreign Government Bonds Issued in the United States	52
11	Default Index, 11 Banking Houses, 1920-1930	55
12	Timing and Quality of Foreign Government Bond Issues Initiated by 11 Banking Houses	57
13	Foreign Government Bonds and Domestic Securities Issued in the United States, and Domestic Bond Yields	88
14	Default Status, at the Close of 1937, of Foreign Government Bonds Issued in the United States	90
15	Default Index Based on Number of Foreign Government Bonds Issued in the United States, 1920-1930	92
16	Average Size of Issue, 'Sound' and 'Unsound' Foreign Government Bonds Issued in the United States	93
17	Default Status of Foreign Government Bonds Issued in the United States by Geographic Areas	94
18	Risk Premiums on Foreign Government Bonds Issued in the United States	95
19	Uncorrected Default Index of Foreign Government Bonds Issued in the United States	96

CHART

1	Foreign Government Bonds Issued in the United States, 1920-1930	11
2	Domestic Bond Issues, Bond Yields, and Foreign Government Bonds Issued in the United States, 1920-1930	21
3	Domestic Common Stocks and Foreign Government Bonds Issued in the United States, 1920-1930	25
4	Sound and Total Foreign Government Bonds Issued in the United States, 1920-1930	32
5	Default Index: Foreign Government Bonds Issued in the United States, 1920-1930	37
6	Default Index Based on Number of Issues, Foreign Government Bonds Issued in the United States, 1920-1930	39
7	Average Price on December 31, 1937 of Defaulted Foreign Government Bonds Issued in the United States, by Time of Issue, 1920-1930	42
8	Foreign Government Bonds Issued in the United States, by Geographic Areas, 1920-1924 and 1925-1929	53
9	Risk Premiums on Foreign Government Bonds Issued in the United States, and Default Index, 1920-1930	61

Introduction

1 Current Opinions on Foreign Lending

The United States is now entering its second major period of foreign lending. It is, at present, the only country with the capacity for large scale foreign investment with private or public funds, and the greater part of the world needs its economic aid. The resumption of foreign lending creates a host of problems, political and economic, which are being widely discussed. This study does not deal directly with these problems. We treat only past experience but hope that by re-opening the past and by presenting what happened in a new light we may contribute indirectly to the understanding of current problems.

Probably most economists agree that the United States should export capital.[1] However, except for purely political loans, this is considered desirable only on the assumption that foreign lending will be more successful than in the twenties, that the investors' sad

---

[1] To quote only a few representative opinions:

"A progressive, dynamic world economy on a multilateral basis cannot be reconstructed without the resumption of productive foreign investment." Report of the Committee on Foreign Economic Relations, appointed by the Twentieth Century Fund (Norman S. Buchanan and Friedrich A. Lutz, *Rebuilding the World Economy*, 1947), p. 305.

"On the basis of the replies received it may be said that economists believe that a reasonably large outflow of capital is desirable for broad economic and political reasons. About 90 percent of the replies support this view." Results of a poll conducted by a Committee of the American Economic Association, Papers and Proceedings, May 1946, p. 240.

"In the world such as we find it foreign long-term lending is another essential prerequisite for the successful operation of a stable international currency system." Ragnar Nurkse, *International Currency Experience* (League of Nations, 1944), p. 202.

"It is both natural and logical that American capital should resume investment activity abroad." H. B. Lary, *The United States in the World Economy* (Department of Commerce, Economic Series No. 23, 1943), p. 19.

experience with foreign loans will not be repeated.[2] Will this be possible and how can it be achieved? The answer depends partly upon one's interpretation of the past.

According to widespread popular opinion almost all the American money invested in foreign loans has been lost. Experts know, of course, that this is not true. In their excellent and comprehensive investigation of foreign lending J. T. Madden, Marcus Nadler, and Harry Sauvain find: "The fact is that interest has been paid in full, through the longest and most severe depression of modern times, on almost two-thirds of all the foreign bonds currently [December 1935] outstanding."[3] Although losses on foreign bonds were smaller than generally believed they were large enough to constitute a grave problem. Investors cannot be encouraged to buy foreign bonds again unless there is reason to expect that the outcome will be better. What are the chances for such an improvement?

The answers experts offer differ according to the factors they hold mainly responsible for past defaults and their views on the possibility and probability of removing or controlling such factors in the future. Many factors conducive to defaults on foreign loans have been revealed and discussed, factors so numerous and powerful that the reader is sometimes surprised to find that two-thirds of all loans remained safe and sound after all.

First, there are factors inherent in the loans themselves. A large number of foreign loans, undoubtedly, were mistaken *ex ante,* i.e., had they been carefully weighed in the light of then prevailing

---

[2] "The world would do well to avoid, even at considerable cost, another debacle of defaults and repudiations, replete with recriminations and strained relationships, such as followed upon the last upswing in American foreign lending in the twenties." Norman Buchanan, *International Investment and Domestic Welfare* (Holt, 1945), p. 120.

"To establish a sounder foundation for foreign lending in future is therefore one of the two or three most important reforms the world needs. . . ." Sir Arthur Salter, *Recovery* (London, 1931), p. 128.

[3] *America's Experience as Creditor Nation* (Prentice Hall, 1937), p. 136. See also Cleona Lewis, *America's Stake in International Investments* (Brookings Institution, 1938), p. 398: "Of the existing foreign bonds that were originally issued here during the prosperous twenties, around 35 to 40 per cent are now [1935] in default."

conditions they would never have been granted. Second, other loans were basically sound, and were defaulted only because of the sudden termination of foreign lending and the general depression. These have been termed bad investments *ex post*.[4] The factors responsible for *ex ante* bad loans have frequently been deemed relatively unimportant. "Under the combined influence of the fall in business activity and in prices, the imposition of the tariff of 1930, and the cessation of new foreign investment, the total amount of dollars paid out by the United States to foreign countries fell from 7,400 million dollars in 1929 to only 2,400 millions in 1932. At the same time foreign countries had contractual debt-service payments of some 900 millions due to the United States each year. Under such circumstances it was inevitable that many of these obligations should be defaulted. By comparison with the magnitude of these strains, all other explanations of the relatively unsatisfactory outcome of the past foreign lending experience of the United States must be of distinctly secondary significance. It is for this reason that I have not attempted to appraise in detail the results of this experience in analyzing future possibilities. . . ."[5]

This emphasis on the transfer problem leads to the view that the success of future loans is predicated on two conditions: American capital must be exported at a stable rate in order to prevent sudden reversals in the balance of payments of debtor countries; and American imports must be expanded in order to assure the service of new foreign loans through an adequate supply of dollars. Opinions differ as to whether these conditions will be met in the future.

2 Nature of the Study

We approach foreign lending from a different angle. Rather than focus attention on the economic conditions prevailing when foreign

---

[4] See Ragnar Nurkse, *Internationale Kapitalbewegungen* (Vienna, 1935), p. 210. For an enumeration of factors inherent in the loans themselves see, e.g., Cleona Lewis, op. cit., pp. 403-10.

[5] H. B. Lary, American Economic Association, Papers and Proceedings, May 1946, p. 683. See also Madden et al., op. cit., p. 166: "The transfer problem . . . must be regarded as the principal cause of the defaults on foreign dollar bonds during the 1930's." The same view is expressed in *International Capital Movements during the Inter-War Period* (United Nations, 1949).

loans were defaulted, or deal with the impact of the great depression on outstanding loans, we investigate the relation between conditions at the time of issue of the loans and their quality, their ability to stand the test of depression. Defaulted foreign loans have hitherto been analyzed with reference to time of default, type of borrower (government or private), and form of lending (portfolio or direct); the time of lending has virtually been ignored. The customary treatment considers foreign loans as if they had been parts of one great investment project instead of a sequence of individual investments. This is grossly inadequate if the quality of the loans changed drastically.

Current judgments on American experience with the foreign loans of the 1920's might be refined and corrected if more attention were paid to the general economic situation at the time of their issue and its influence on their character and soundness. The main period of foreign lending, 1921-29, was marked by an extraordinary expansion of financial activity, mounting in three successively higher waves and culminating in the 'speculative mania' of 1929. Is it not probable that new foreign loans reflected this? Should we not expect the quality of foreign loans to change during such a period, to deteriorate as speculation increased and the boom swelled? And if it did change in any considerable degree would not that affect our judgment and evaluation of the experience with foreign lending?

Though we deal exclusively with American foreign lending, the analysis may have a wider bearing. As far as we know, fluctuations in the quality of new investments of any kind have seldom been investigated empirically. One exception is R. J. Saulnier's study of urban mortgage loans. Another is G. W. Edwards' analysis of domestic bonds. Both studies are described more fully in Chapter 2. Otherwise, although business failures and defaults have been related to various factors, including conditions at the time of failure, little if any attention had been paid to conditions at the time of investment.

Yet fluctuations in investment quality appear to be relevant to the understanding of economic change, particularly the business cycle. Deterioration in investment quality may be one of the factors

INTRODUCTION

implicit in such terms as 'over-optimism', 'reckless speculation', 'boom psychology'. It may prove to be one of the maladjustments that, as in Wesley C. Mitchell's or Gottfried Haberler's theories of the business cycle, develop during expansion and contribute to the downturn.

More specifically, decline in investment quality between 1921 and 1929 would fit well into Arthur F. Burns' and Wesley C. Mitchell's hypothesis regarding major cycles,[6] this period being the expansion phase of one of these major cycles. Their argument runs as follows: "After a severe depression industrial activity rebounds sharply, but speculation does not. The following contraction in business is mild, which leads people to be less cautious. Consequently, in the next two or three cycles, while the cyclical advances become progressively smaller in industrial activity, they become progressively larger in speculative activity. Finally, the speculative boom collapses and a drastic liquidation follows, which ends this cycle of cycles and brings us back to the starting point." When people become "less cautious" the proportion of unsound investments is likely to increase in various fields.

As an instance of explicit reference to the deterioration of new investments, we may note J. A. Schumpeter's discussion of cyclical expansions, which are characterized in his view by the development of "reckless, fraudulent, or otherwise unsuccessful enterprise, which cannot stand the tests administered by recession."[7] The importance Schumpeter attributed to this factor is evident in his diagnosis of the great depression: "I submit that, given ... depressive tendency and supernormal sensitivity, the following facts constitute adequate explanation of the 'disaster' in the United States.

The first fact is the speculative mania of 1927-29. . . . The second fact was the weakness of the United States banking system. . . . Third in importance was the mortgage situation, both urban and rural. Again I maintain that its most serious features were entirely due to reckless borrowing and lending; that is to say, to

[6] Arthur F. Burns and Wesley C. Mitchell, *Measuring Business Cycles* (NBER, 1946), p. 460.
[7] *Business Cycles* (McGraw-Hill, 1939), I, 148.

avoidable deviations from normal business practice. The explanatory value for the crisis of this element is ten times as great as that of the most elegant difference equation."[8]

Extensive investigation would, of course, be required to obtain measurements of quality fluctuations in major fields of investment. By endeavoring to obtain some new insights into one historical experience, the foreign lending of the twenties, we hope to make a modest contribution to such a broad collection of evidence.

3 Some Remarks on Our Findings

The statistical analysis in Chapter 2 shows how greatly the quality of new foreign issues, as measured by the proportion that subsequently defaulted, deteriorated during the 11 years 1920-30. For example, only 6 percent of the issues of 1920 went to borrowers who defaulted in the 1930's while 63 percent of those of 1928 suffered this fate; and of all loans issued in the 5 years, 1920-24, only 18 percent went to borrowers who defaulted in the 1930's while for 1925-29 the ratio is as high as 50 percent.

If we consider the impact of unsound loans upon sound ones it is even more striking that issues of the early twenties fared so much better in the crisis than later issues. "Supposing . . . that a modest and useful loan had already been issued to, and on the credit of, a particular country, and utilized for the most productive purposes; the subscriber would still lose if later and wasteful loans disorganized the public finances [of the borrowing country] and compelled default."[9] Among the defaulted issues of the early twenties some "modest and useful" loans were doubtless defaulted because of later wasteful ones. Consequently, the difference between the outcome of early and that of later loans reflects only a part of the difference in their original qualities. It is the more significant that 82 percent of the loans of the early period remained sound.

The big variations in loan quality and the satisfactory outcome of early loans cannot be explained by transfer difficulties, since

[8] The Decade of the Twenties, American Economic Association, Papers and Proceedings, May 1946, pp. 8-10.
[9] Salter, op. cit., p. 123.

INTRODUCTION 7

dollar scarcity in the thirties affected loans of 1920 as much as those of 1928. Nor can they be explained by the other factors held responsible for adverse results of American foreign lending, such as: "our ineptness at this type of business",[10] "the very nature of capital accumulation with the assistance of foreign borrowing", etc.[11] Factors that might explain the adverse results of lending in general do not suffice to explain differences in the outcome of loans issued at different times. They must originate in other forces which have so far received less attention.

The evaluation of American experience with foreign lending may be modified by our findings. One group of experts indicts the granting of credits between the two world wars as a complete mistake; another deems it on the whole sound and reasonable and holds the great depression solely responsible for its failure. Both views must be corrected if most foreign loans floated in the early years after World War I were sound and most of the mistakes were made in the later twenties, abnormal years in many respects. In the future it might be possible to improve results of foreign lending by applying the methods of the past successful times while avoiding as far as possible those of the years of unsuccessful lending.

[10] Wesley C. Mitchell, NBER, *24th Annual Report,* 1944, p. 26.
[11] Buchanan, op. cit., p. 116.

Chapter 1

THE VOLUME OF FOREIGN LENDING

1 *Scope of the Investigation*

Our analysis is confined to foreign loans issued during the brief span of 11 years, 1920-30. The limits are set by the short history of American foreign lending.

Until the close of the 19th century "The flotation of foreign securities in the United States was a rare event".[1] The United States was almost exclusively an importer of capital. With the turn of the century the shift from international debtor to international creditor began; American investors became interested in foreign securities. Between 1900 and 1905 there was even a sort of miniature boom in foreign underwriting. However, until World War I foreign lending was on so small a scale that it presented no major problems and attracted little attention. The big change took place during World War I; 1915 was the first year of large scale foreign underwriting by the United States (Table 1). In one single war year, 1916, the par value of foreign dollar loan flotations exceeded that in the preceding 15 years. The magnitude of the change can be seen by comparing the two 15-year periods, 1900-14 and 1915-29. The total number of foreign issues was 273 in the former, 1,936 in the latter; the corresponding par values increased from $1,132 million to $13,742 million. In view of the small scale of American lending before 1915 we exclude it from our analysis. World War I is omitted for another reason — the abnormal character of the loans, the majority of which went to Great Britain and France, and must be regarded as a form of American participation in the war. Since 67 percent of foreign loans in 1919 still went to the British and Canadian governments, this year also has been excluded.

[1] Department of Commerce, *Handbook on American Underwriting of Foreign Securities* by Ralph A. Young, Trade Promotion Series, No. 104, 1930, p. 9.

Table 1

Total Foreign Dollar Capital Issues, Governmental and Private
Publicly Offered in the United States

Year of Issue	Number of Issues	Amount ($ million)	Year of Issue	Number of Issues	Amount ($ million)
1900-13 (an. av.)	18	78	1923	76	498
			1924	120	1,217
1914	26	45	1925	164	1,316
1915	80	818			
1916	102	1,160	1926	230	1,288
1917	65	720	1927	265	1,577
1918	28	23	1928	221	1,489
1919	65	771			
			1929	148	706
1920	104	603	1930	122	1,088
1921	116	692			
1922	152	863			

Department of Commerce, *Handbook on American Underwriting of Foreign Securities* by Ralph A. Young, Trade Promotion Series, No. 104, 1930, pp. 10, 11; figures for 1930, Department of Commerce, *Trade Information Bulletin*, No. 746.

The end of our period is likewise set by the history of foreign lending. The peak of foreign underwriting was reached in the first half of 1928; foreign issues then declined and, after a short-lived recovery in the first half of 1930, came to a complete standstill in 1931 when the era of defaults began. During the rest of the interwar period only an insignificant number of foreign loans, largely for refunding purposes, were granted.

This investigation deals solely with foreign government bonds, the most important among the foreign loans of this period. It is based upon an itemized record of foreign government, state or provincial, and municipal issues, including governmentally guaranteed or controlled corporate issues, publicly offered in the United States. This record, the only comprehensive monthly list of foreign security flotations ever issued, was compiled by the Department of Commerce and published in 1930 in its *Handbook on American Underwriting of Foreign Securities*.[2]

We have excluded a few categories from the government and government controlled securities listed in the *Handbook*: loans to

[2] Lists for subsequent years are published annually in the Department's *Trade Information Bulletin*. No such record has been compiled in Great Britain despite its long history of foreign lending.

American non-contiguous territories and possessions; loans with a term of less than 2 years;[3] and 5 small issues of common and preferred stock which the *Handbook* calls "minor exceptions". Our measures of quality, yield, etc. are designed for and applicable to bonds only. Altogether the loans omitted on these three counts are 18 percent of the total number and 9 percent of the dollar value of government and government controlled loans listed in the *Handbook*.

In short, our investigation covers European, Latin American, Canadian, and Far Eastern government and government guaranteed or controlled bonds with terms of 2 years or more, publicly offered in the United States during 1920-30. Within this definition we deal with a 100 percent sample, i.e., with all such bonds listed in the *Handbook*[4] comprising about 800 issues of 43 borrowing countries with a total par value of a little over $7 billion. As a rule our analysis refers to the nominal dollar amount, not to the number of issues. For this purpose the dollar amount of a loan is the par value of the part of the issue that was actually underwritten in the United States.

Some doubts attach to the inclusion of Canadian bonds among foreign loans. American investors in the 1920's hardly looked upon Canada as a foreign country. Geographic proximity, the interlacing of the Canadian and American economies, and familiarity of American investors with Canadian conditions sets off Canadian from all other foreign investments. As the results of our analysis might be considerably affected by the treatment of Canadian bonds, accounting as they do for about 21 percent of the dollar value and for about 44 percent of the number of all the bonds in our lists, we analyze foreign loans both including and excluding Canadian securities.

The series of bond flotations here discussed represents the basic data for which we derive an index of loan quality in Chapter 2. However, before proceeding to this, our major objective, we want

[3] Loans with a term of less than 10 years were few; most issues had maturities of 10 to 40 years.
[4] A few errors found in the *Handbook,* such as the listing of an issue which was withdrawn, were corrected.

to examine this series itself, since it reveals some interesting facts about foreign lending.

2 Cycles in Foreign Lending

Three cycles in the dollar amount of foreign bond flotations stand out clearly (Chart 1).[5] Their contours are so smooth that we can identify the turning points without hesitation. Loan cycles move counter to general business with almost perfect synchronism. The

[5] All moving averages presented in this study are 4-quarter moving averages centered by 2-item moving averages. The highly erratic character of the series makes smoothing desirable, though moving averages have the disadvantage of reducing the amplitude of fluctuation and may affect the turning points also. Actually, however, peaks and troughs in the moving averages differ at most by one quarter from the turning points in the seasonally adjusted data (cf. Chart 1).

Chart 1
**Foreign Government Bonds Issued in the United States
1920 – 1930**

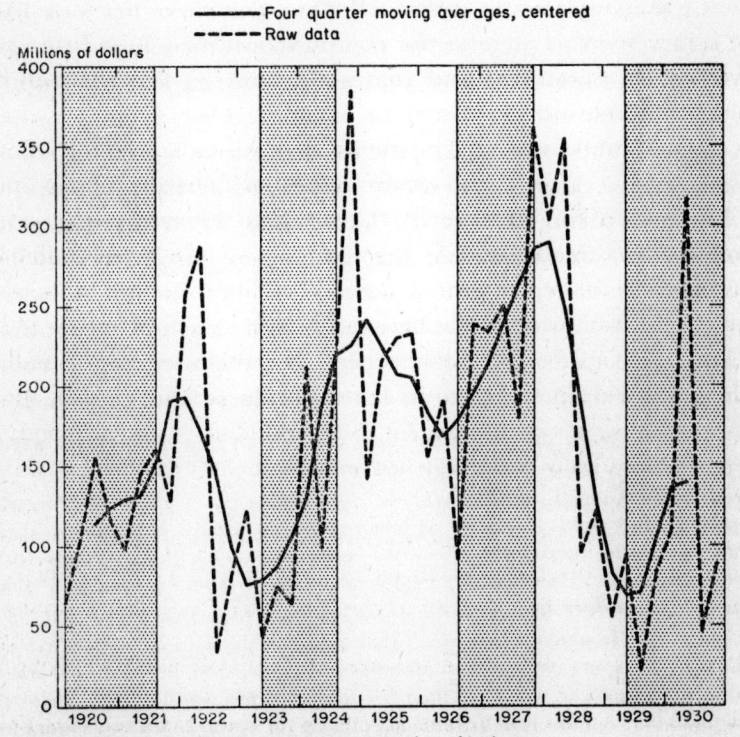

Shaded areas represent contractions, white areas, expansions of business cycles according to NBER chronology. Appendix Table 13.

sole deviations are near the turning points. The loan curve lags one or two quarters at business cycle troughs and leads by one quarter at business cycle peaks, except in 1929 when the turning points coincide.[6]

This shape and timing of the loan curve, its close relation to cycles in general domestic business activity, is quite surprising for several reasons. First, as relatively few issues are included in the loan curve, considerable random fluctuations might be expected despite the moving averages. Second, the issuing of securities in general has been found to be a "highly volatile process" conforming ill to business cycles.[7] Third, foreign bond issues are inversely related to business cycles, and inverted series as a class conform less well than positive series.[8] Finally, 'erratic' is the term most frequently applied to the foreign lending of the twenties and we are used to hearing the movements of international capital described as 'senseless and irrational'. Does our curve not look like the achievement of an office for contracyclical planning of foreign investments, expanding and contracting foreign loans promptly as domestic business contracts or expands? One might say that the United States was developing its new role as a creditor country in the intervals between expansions in its internal economy.

Another striking feature of the series is the trend that runs through the three cycles. As the direction of foreign borrowing was inversely related to general business activity, one might expect that this relation would hold between as well as within cycles; that is, one might expect the highest peak of foreign lending to coincide with the deepest trough in general business, and so forth. But

[6] In evaluating leads and lags in flotations the lapse of time between the negotiation and flotation of a loan must be kept in mind.

[7] Wesley C. Mitchell, *What Happens during Business Cycles — a Progress Report* (NBER, 1951), Ch. 6. Mitchell ranks 29 groups of series by their conformity to business cycles. Security issues are among the 6 groups with lowest conformity. However, the conformity of some types of issue, e.g., common stocks, is rather high.

[8] Ibid., p. 96. "In general, influences that tend to repress an activity in expansion encounter more opposition than influences favoring an increase, and when repressing influences win out, their victories are less regular from cycle to cycle than the victories won by influences that push upward. *Mutatis mutandis,* the like holds true in contraction."

for the most part the reverse was true. The second trough of our curve is not half as deep as the first and each peak is considerably higher than the preceding; at the same time domestic business too rose in successive waves. In other words, though foreign loans moved inversely to business cycles they had the same rising trend. Evidently, the increase in the volume of credit from one cycle to the next was large enough to allow for the expansion of both domestic and foreign lending.[9]

Applying the concept of the major cycle to the three successively rising waves of the 1920's, the foreign loan series may be described also as being positively related to major and inversely to minor cycles in general business.

3 *The Balance of Payments and Foreign Bond Cycles*

Fluctuations in the amount of lending are not our subject. However, the cycles in the foreign bond series are too intriguing to be passed without a few comments on how they might be interpreted. Their relation to the balance of payments is of major interest. Were the cycles in foreign lending determined by cycles in the trade balance?

The main features of the American balance of payments in the 1920's were roughly these: imports moved consistently and exports usually with American business cycles, but since the swings of imports had larger amplitudes the export surplus moved inversely to business cycles. In expansions imports increased more than exports and the export surplus shrank; in contractions imports fell more than exports and the surplus grew.

These inverse cycles in the trade balance were very roughly paralleled by cycles in the net outflow of long term capital which also fell when domestic business improved and rose when domestic business contracted. Thus equilibrium in the balance of payments was at least partly maintained by parallel changes in the net outflow of goods and capital. This in itself is, of course, not surprising. We expect net capital exports to be accompanied by a favorable balance of trade. What is puzzling is the mechanism of the adjust-

[9] "The total [expansion of bank credit] was sufficient to finance a large export of capital and an enormous increase in our domestic capital equipment", J. M. Clark, *Strategic Factors in Business Cycles* (NBER, 1934), p. 99.

ment process. Precisely in what way, by what process of transmission did flows of goods and of capital influence each other?

Several answers have been offered. They concern us only as far as they throw light on the fluctuations in the large part of capital movements we investigate: bond issues.

Arthur I. Bloomfield in his excellent, thorough examination of the Mechanism of Adjustment of the American Balance of Payments: 1919-29, discards the possibility that foreign bond flotations were determined by the trade balance: "We neglect, as highly unlikely, the possibility that the parallelism was the result of a mechanism of adjustment sequence *from* the trade balance *to* the long term capital balance."[10] At present, when borrowing is so largely determined by balance of payment deficits, this summary rejection may not seem justified. However, it must not be forgotten that conditions in the twenties were different. State or municipal governments, as far as they needed foreign exchange at all, could buy it freely. And even national governments were usually not motivated by balance of payments difficulties when they decided to borrow abroad. The gaps the government wanted to fill with foreign loans were in their domestic budgets, not in their balance of payments; funds were sought abroad for rebuilding or developing transportation and industry because investment capital was relatively short and expensive at home.

To this it may be objected that the American trade balance may have affected foreign borrowers indirectly through its influence on credit policies in debtor countries. The following hypothesis seems logical: when Americans bought more abroad, pressure on monetary reserves in debtor countries was eased and credit was more readily available, thereby reducing the incentive to borrow in the United States. A drop in American imports, on the other hand, increased trade deficits and pressure on reserves, and induced foreign governments to seek abroad the money it was harder to raise at home. Thus the inverse cycles of American capital exports would be explained simply and plausibly by the positive cycles of American merchandise imports.

But a glance at trade figures shows that Bloomfield was right in rejecting this line of reasoning. Exports of individual debtor

[10] *Quarterly Journal of Economics,* May 1943, p. 344.

nations did not fluctuate with total American imports; hence it is hardly conceivable that our imports were decisive for the credit policies of these countries. Nor did borrowings of individual countries, except possibly Canada, show any clear relation to American imports.

Yet cycles in foreign trade might cause cycles in bond issues in another way: through their impact on the credit situation in the lending country. William Adams Brown, Jr. offers this interpretation of British lending in the 19th century: "Net exports of goods, services and securities increase both the foreign assets and domestic deposits of the banks. Banks whose foreign assets accumulate too rapidly attempt to replace them by domestic assets, which contributes to easy money in the home market. A connection is thus established between the current accumulation of foreign credits through trade by a country having an international money market and the creation of favorable conditions in that market for the placement of foreign loans."[11]

But Brown does not think this interpretation applicable to the United States. "The capacity of the New York market to extend long term credit was great, but the economic connections between the volume of savings available for lending abroad and the character of the country's foreign trade were very loose."[11] The fact that dollar bond issues turned up at or before business cycle peaks, which are typically not periods of easy money, also contradicts this explanation.[12] Thus it seems unlikely that the cycles in American foreign bond issues were caused by cyclical changes of the trade balance.

4 Foreign Business Cycles and Bond Cycles

a) CYCLES IN DEBTOR COUNTRIES

Foreign economic and political conditions might be supposed to be the salient factors in fluctuations of foreign lending. There is, indeed, a strong presumption that they were. J. W. Angell has advanced an interesting hypothesis along this line with respect to American net capital exports in the 1920's. He suggests that

[11] *The International Gold Standard Reinterpreted* (NBER, 1940), pp. 558-9.
[12] Since foreign flotations in Great Britain, as distinguished from net capital exports, also show a pattern inverted to British business cycles, some doubts attach to the validity of this explanation even for Great Britain.

changes in commodity and capital movements have been, "directly or indirectly, the common results of a common antecedent condition, the fluctuating state of economic affairs in Europe".[13] He thinks that American net capital exports were inversely related to fluctuations in European business, i.e., that they fell as Europe recovered from the war and again as it recovered from the stabilization crisis of 1924.

Similar reasoning might apply to foreign bond flotations and to non-European countries. We try to test this hypothesis by comparing fluctuations in the dollar bond issues of a few major borrowing countries with their own business cycles. The analysis is confined to the 8 countries in our bond records whose business fluctuations have been described from a viewpoint that warrants comparison with the data on American cycles used here: Argentina, Australia, Austria, Brazil, Germany, France, Italy, and the Netherlands.[14] Even these data on foreign cycles are probably less reliable and are certainly less precise than those on American cycles.

The discontinuous nature of foreign borrowing by governments presents another difficulty. Whereas all foreign bond issues in the United States form a continuous series, the individual foreign country's dollar issues were intermittent even for the heaviest borrowers and came at wide intervals for the others. Consequently, results might vary materially, depending upon whether a particular quarter is or is not included in a cycle phase. To increase the reliability of the test we mark off cycle phases in three ways. First, we compare issues floated during the 3 quarters centered on business cycle peaks with those during the 3 quarters centered on troughs (Method A); second, issues during 5 quarters centered on peaks are compared with those during 5 quarters centered on troughs (Method B); and finally, issues floated in quarters nearer peaks are compared with those in quarters nearer troughs (Method C). The last method includes all the issues for each country in the analysis. But however the comparison is made, no consistent

[13] Equilibrium in International Trade: The United States, 1919-26, *Quarterly Journal of Economics*, May 1928, p. 432.
[14] W. L. Thorp, *Business Annals* (NBER, 1926); NBER *News-Bulletin 43* (1932); Burns and Mitchell, op. cit., pp. 78, 79 (for France and Germany).

Table 2
Foreign Government Bonds Issued in the United States Compared with Business Cycles in the Borrowing Country and in the United States, 1920-1930

AVERAGE AMOUNT ISSUED PER QUARTER DURING PEAK AND TROUGH PERIODS IN BUSINESS CYCLES OF BORROWING COUNTRIES

	Method A		Method B		Method C	
ISSUING COUNTRY	Peak period	Trough period	Peak period	Trough period	Peak period	Trough period
			(millions of dollars)			
Argentina	5	20	9	19	10	14
Australia	7	4	7	2	6	4
Austria	0	1	0	1	3	3
Brazil	8	12	8	14	6	14
France	22	14	14	15	11	12
Germany	16	15	30	22	35	25
Italy	3	0	9	0	7	1
Netherlands	0	0	0	5	1	6
Total	61	66	77	78	79	79

AVERAGE AMOUNT ISSUED PER QUARTER DURING PEAK AND TROUGH PERIODS IN BUSINESS CYCLES IN THE UNITED STATES

Total, 8 countries	32	111	34	102	45	96
Total, all countries	103	220	111	219	119	217

See text for description of methods of defining peak and trough periods.

cyclical pattern emerges. While Australia, Germany and Italy borrowed chiefly at times when they enjoyed relatively high business activity, Argentina, Brazil, and the Netherlands floated most of their issues during periods when their economics were relatively depressed. Austrian issues were about equal in the two periods; for France the results are inconclusive. Together the 8 countries' issues at their respective cycle peaks were, depending on the definition of peaks and troughs used, either equal to or only slightly smaller than those at their troughs.

The contrast between these results and those obtained when foreign issues are compared with cycles in American business is striking. Whether we compare issues at peaks with those at troughs, or issues during the entire upper half with those during the entire lower half of the cycle, whether we deal with all bonds or only with those issued by the 8 countries, we invariably find that foreign lending was much greater during American depressions than during American prosperity. For all the loans in our record the average amount issued during the 3 quarters centered at peaks of American business cycles was $103 million; at troughs, $220 million. For the 8 countries the contrast is even greater: $32 million at peaks and $111 million at troughs. In view of the fact that the 8 countries issued an average of $61 million in quarters when their own business was at peak level and an average of $66 million in quarters when their own business was depressed, the conclusion seems warranted that American business conditions were the dominant factor.

The explanation of the lack of relationship between fluctuations in foreign issues floated in the United States and foreign business cycles, of the fact that some countries borrowed primarily when they enjoyed relatively prosperous business conditions, that others sought loans more frequently when their business was depressed, and that the issues of a third group were about equal in the two periods, may be, in part at least, that we deal with government issues. As governments, even states and municipalities, are motivated in their borrowings largely by nonbusiness factors, the absence of cyclical conformity is not surprising.[15] What has to be explained is the close relationship between their borrowings in this country and business conditions here.

b) CYCLES IN FOREIGN CREDITOR COUNTRIES

The influence of business swings in borrowing countries on borrowers' decisions cannot explain the fluctuations in American foreign lending; but what about the effect of business cycles in foreign creditor countries on their competitive position? If the cost of borrowing moves differently in foreign creditor countries and in the United States, borrowers may shift from one market to another and this may partly account for the cycles in American bond flotations. The only major lender to compete with New York in the interwar period was London. Did variations in interest rate differentials between the two markets govern American foreign lending?

In Great Britain an embargo placed on foreign loans during the war was not withdrawn until the end of 1925. Until then the

[15] "As might be expected, the loans applied for by governments show but a slight degree of coordination with business cycles." Wesley C. Mitchell, *Business Cycles* (University of California Press, 1913), p. 405.

amount of lending depended largely upon the stringency of its enforcement. Moreover, the Bank of England controlled the quantity and direction of foreign lending during the entire period, discriminating between different classes of borrowers and types of loan. In consequence some borrowers found terms more favorable in London than in New York while the contrary held for others. As variations in London's role as capital exporter depended much more upon changes in policy than upon interest rates we must not look to the latter for a measure of the role of British lending. Data on the volume of British loans are more revealing because they reflect variations in the application of direct controls as well as in costs (Table 3).

Table 3

Foreign Government Securities Issued in the United Kingdom and in the United States, 1920-1930

Year of Issue	U. K.[a] (£ mil.)	U. S.[b] ($ mil.)	Year of Issue	U. K.[a] (£ mil.)	U. S.[b] ($ mil.)
1920	12.0	439	1925	33.8	818
1921	84.6	532	1926	56.0	673
1922	87.1	660	1927	78.2	973
1923	94.4	304	1928	71.9	875
1924	100.2	912	1929	34.7	253
			1930	68.8	650

[a] New Capital Issues to British Overseas and Foreign Public Authorities: Midland Bank, *Monthly Review*. In contrast to the American series the British series includes stock issues and is based on prices of issues.

[b] Foreign government and government guaranteed bonds of a term of 2 years or more, publicly offered in the United States. Adapted from Department of Commerce *Handbook on American Underwriting of Foreign Securities* (1930), pp. 75-132.

Since foreign government bond issues in Great Britain move in the same direction as those in the United States in 7 out of 9 years, variations in the impact of British competition can hardly explain the ups and downs in American foreign lending. During the 1924-26 contraction in American lending British foreign issues dropped sharply because of the strict embargo placed on such issues preparatory to Britain's return to the gold standard. The steep decline in dollar bond issues in the second half of 1928 (Chart 1) also was accompanied by a decline in British foreign issues. In 1923, however, British issues did rise while American fell 54 percent. It is quite likely that in this case some of the financing that would have been carried in the United States market was done in London, especially as interest rates declined in Britain and rose slightly in the United States. But even here the importance of this factor should not be overrated. A $356 million drop in American issues from 1922 to 1923 evidently cannot be explained by the $35 million rise in British issues.[16]

5 *American Business Cycles and Foreign Bond Cycles*

a) CYCLES IN DOMESTIC BOND ISSUES

The foregoing points to American business cycles as the main cause of fluctuations in dollar bond flotations. But how did the swings in American business exert their influence? What precisely caused foreign issues to decline when domestic business expanded and to increase when it slumped?

The obvious answer is to attribute the inverse cycles to the bond character of the loans. Both H. B. Lary and Arthur I. Bloomfield, noting that total foreign capital issues (including government and corporate bonds and also stock issues) moved inversely to business cycles, advanced this explanation tentatively and with reservations. Bloomfield found that foreign flotations were "inversely correlated with domestic activity in seven years of the [ten-year] period. . . . Inasmuch as most foreign flotations in the United States were bonds, it is likely that they may have shared the same fate as domestic bond issues, which likewise tended to be inversely correlated with business conditions. Certainly the drastic decline of foreign flotations late in 1928 and in 1929 seems clearly to have been associated in large part with the sharp shift of investment and speculative interest away from bond issues of all sorts, and it is possible that this same factor may also have been an important element in accounting for the inverse behavior of foreign flotations to domestic activity in the earlier years of the period".[17]

To what degree did foreign government bond offerings behave like domestic bond offerings? Chart 2 reveals considerable similarity in the movements of the two series. In 31 of the 39 quarter to

---

[16] Brown, op. cit., p. 328: "The very small figures for [British] loans in the last months of the year [1923] . . . reflected the foreign exchange crisis and the flight from the pound."

[17] Op. cit., pp. 367-8.

THE VOLUME OF FOREIGN LENDING 21

Chart 2
Domestic Bond Issues, Bond Yields, and Foreign Government Bonds Issued in the United States, 1920-1930

——— Domestic Bond Issues (scale at left)
- - - - Foreign Government Bond Issues (scale at right)
········· Yield on 30 High Grade Corporate Bonds (scale at right)

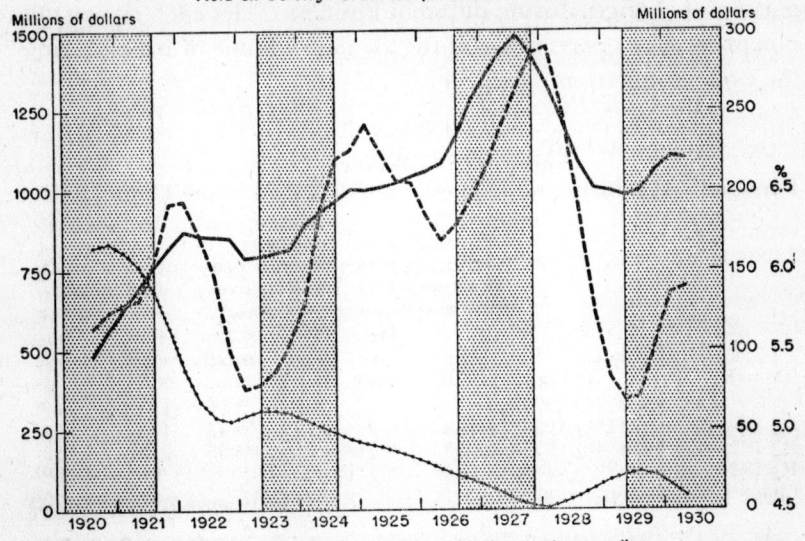

Shaded areas represent contractions, white areas, expansions of business cycles according to NBER chronology. Four quarter moving averages, centered; Appendix Table 13.

quarter changes foreign and domestic bond offerings move in the same direction. Three of the six turning points coincide, and a fourth is roughly synchronous. There are, however, significant deviations. Curiously, domestic issues were not as closely related to business cycles as foreign issues. They continued to rise or declined only moderately in two of the three cyclical expansions. During the first business expansion foreign issues fell 61 percent, domestic issues only 10 percent; during the second upswing domestic issues continued to increase, though at a retarded pace, so that foreign issues, which at their peak in the first quarter of 1925, had amounted to 24 percent of domestic issues dropped to 15½ percent of the latter in the second quarter of 1926. Thus it cannot be said that foreign bond issues simply followed the path of domestic issues.

Similarities and dissimilarities of fluctuations in new foreign and domestic bond issues can be described more precisely by comparing the volume of issues during successive peaks and troughs of general business. The differences between the standings at successive turning points measure the rise or fall of the series during an expansion or contraction in general business. To facilitate comparison of changes during different business cycles each rise or fall is expressed as a percentage of the average volume of issues during the cycle in question (Table 4).[18]

Table 4
Conformity to Business Cycles
Foreign Government and Domestic Bonds Issued in the United States

BUSINESS CYCLE			CHANGE DURING EXPANSION IN PERCENT OF CYCLE AVERAGE		CHANGE DURING CONTRACTION IN PERCENT OF CYCLE AVERAGE		CYCLE AVERAGE IN $ MILLION PER QUARTER	
Trough	Peak	Trough	Foreign bonds	Domestic bonds	Foreign bonds	Domestic bonds	Foreign bonds	Domestic bonds
	1Q 1920	3Q 1921			+72[a]	+56[a]	134[a]	717[a]
3Q 1921	2Q 1923	3Q 1924	−88	−2	+133	+43	133	852
3Q 1924	3Q 1926	4Q 1927	−25	+2	+70	+50	219	1,158
4Q 1927	2Q 1929		−124[b]	−57[b]			206[b]	1,239[b]

[a] Peak to peak cycle, 1920-23.   [b] Peak to peak cycle, 1926-29.

We find again that both domestic and foreign bond flotations were inversely related to business cycles. Both rose steeply during contractions and fell or failed to rise during expansions. But domestic bonds conformed less closely: they failed, or almost failed, to decline in two of the three business expansions.

This curious fact, that foreign bond issues followed the pattern of American business cycles more closely than domestic issues, is confirmed when the behavior of the two series is analyzed in more detail. Based simply on the standings at troughs and peaks, Table 4 does not take any account of what happened during expansion or contraction. To show fully the behavior of a series during the course of the cycle, each cycle may be divided into 9 segments and the average value of the series for each segment calculated.[19]

[18] These measures are based on seasonally adjusted data, not on moving averages. For details of technique see Burns and Mitchell, op. cit., Ch. 2.

[19] Three of the 9 segments center on the initial trough, the peak, and the terminal trough. The other 6 segments are obtained by dividing the expansion and contraction each into three parts as nearly equal as possible without using fractions of a quarter. (For full explanation see Burns and Mitchell, op. cit., pp. 144 ff.)

A cycle is thus described by 9 standings, and comparison of successive standings tells us how consistently the series followed the path of general business. We compute this 9-stage cycle pattern for foreign and domestic bond issues, then compare their stage to stage movements: foreign bonds failed to conform to the inverted cycle pattern in 5 out of the 24 stage to stage movements that comprise the 3 cycles, domestic bonds in 8. The total duration of stage to stage intervals when foreign issues failed to conform was 7 quarters of the 37 quarters covered by the 3 cycles; the corresponding figure for domestic issues was 14 quarters. Clearly, foreign bond issues were more closely related to American business cycles than domestic bond issues.

H. B. Lary, in his analysis of the *United States in the World Economy,* arrives at similar conclusions when he compares total foreign flotations, government plus corporate, with domestic corporate bond issues.[20] "New foreign-bond offerings followed a path roughly parallel to that of new domestic corporate bond issues in the period 1919-31. There were, however, important deviations in the two series, especially in 1923 and in 1928-29, that indicated the operation of forces with special bearing on the volume of foreign issues. . . . The explanation seems to lie in the behavior of long term interest rates, which generally tend to harden in the expansion phase of the business cycle and to decline in times of business contraction, and thus to discourage or encourage, respectively, borrowing by foreign entities. Such behavior was particularly true on the occasions mentioned, in view of the fact that rising interest rates in the United States were not accompanied by equivalent increases in foreign countries, with the result that the comparative advantage of borrowing in the American market was decreased. By contrast, domestic bond issues are not influenced to a similar extent by rising long term interest rates, because such increases are usually accompanied by an accentuated internal demand for capital, resulting from prosperous business conditions, that tends to offset the depressive influence of higher interest rates."

This hypothesis is certainly plausible. Yet the behavior of interest rates in the twenties gives it little support. Lary selects the average yields on 30 high grade corporate bonds (Moody's rating

[20] Op. cit., pp. 92-3.

Aaa) as "most nearly representing the trend in real interest rates in the United States".[21] The downward trend of this index (Chart 2) during most of our period (from the third quarter of 1920 to the first of 1928) corresponds well with the rising trend of foreign loans and may in some degree account for it. But the explanation of the three inverse cycles is a different matter.

Of the three contractions in foreign issues only the last, the collapse of 1928, was accompanied by hardening interest rates. From a trough of 4.51 percent in the first quarter of 1928 the index rises to a peak of 4.73 percent in the third quarter of 1929. This is too modest an advance to explain a decline in lending from $289 to $70 million. But it is at least a move in the direction that Lary's explanation leads us to expect. The sharp drop in foreign lending in 1922-23, however, occurred when interest rates were falling to their lowest point in 5 years. The following modest upturn of interest rates can hardly account for the sharp contraction in foreign lending that had preceded it by half a year. In 1925-26, finally, foreign issues contracted in the face of continually declining interest rates.

Thus the behavior of interest rates as represented by high-grade bond yields explains neither the cycles in foreign bond issues nor their deviations from the behavior of domestic bonds. Replacing moving averages by the raw data would not alter this result.

b) COMMON STOCK ISSUES AND FOREIGN BOND CYCLES

The explanation of the cyclical behavior of bond flotations must be sought in the differentials between expected profits and interest rates, not in interest rates themselves. During an upswing when people are optimistic about profits they invest in stocks, stock prices rise, and it becomes attractive to raise capital by equity financing. But this by no means implies that bond prices must fall. As long as credit expansion furnishes the new money for the stock market and credit policies prevent interest rates from rising, bond prices will hold their own or may even move slightly upward. Flotations of new bonds, however, will drop in such a period as high stock prices make stock issuing more attractive. During the downswing the situation is reversed.

[21] Ibid., p. 96.

THE VOLUME OF FOREIGN LENDING 25

Chart 3
Domestic Common Stocks and Foreign Government Bonds Issued in the United States, 1920–1930

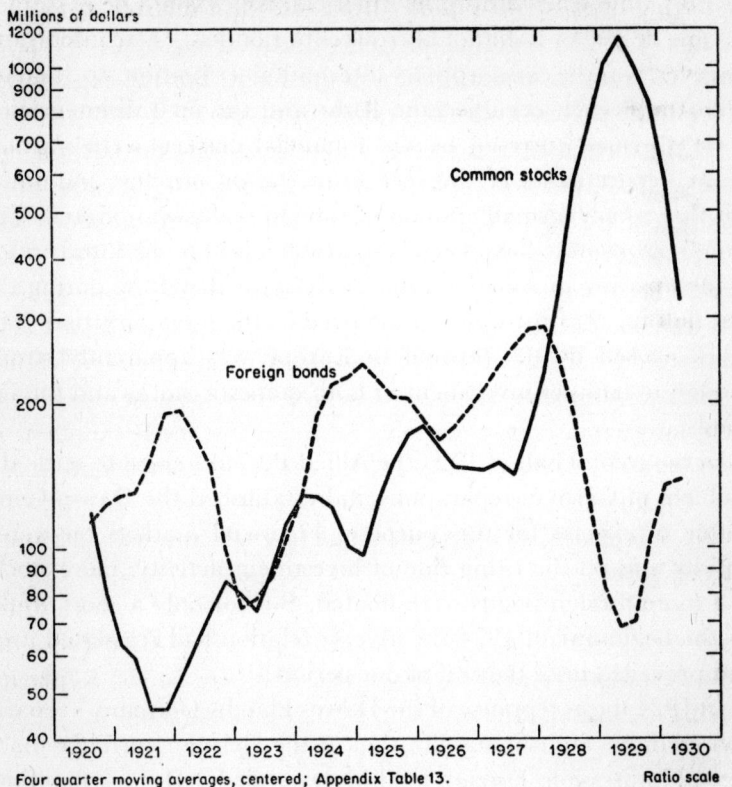

Four quarter moving averages, centered; Appendix Table 13.   Ratio scale

The behavior of new common stock issues is most revealing in this connection. Chart 3 shows their striking inverse relation to foreign bond flotations during the entire period except in one year, 1923. The foreign series lags slightly at some turning points but otherwise mirrors closely the fluctuations in American common stock issues.

In the second half of 1920 and in 1921 the volume of stock issues declined while underwriting of foreign bonds rose despite the unfavorable conditions in most foreign countries. In 1922 stock issues went up and foreign bond issues promptly fell off.

The year 1923 represents the above mentioned exception: both curves first declined, then rose in almost exactly the same fashion.

This is the same year that was found exceptional with respect to relations between British and American issues (see above). It was the only time when a drop in American issues could be explained to some degree by a shift of borrowers to London. More important, however, was the extraordinary international situation. In January 1923 the French occupied the Ruhr and the final disintegration of the German currency began. Financial markets were alarmed by the 'reparations war' between France and Germany, and under this threat only a small amount of foreign bonds was offered. The same reasons may have been responsible also for the interruption to the upswing in American stock offerings; therefore, during the first half of 1923 the two series moved in the same direction. The shock caused by the turmoil in Europe was apparently strong enough to hamper investment in both domestic stocks and foreign bonds.

In the second half of 1923 the Allied Powers agreed to settle the problem of German reparations and established the Dawes Committee of experts for this purpose. Financial markets recovered rapidly and on the rising tide of investment activity, more stocks *and* more foreign bonds were floated. But for only a short while. By the beginning of 1924 the inverse relation had reasserted itself and prevailed until the end of our period.

In 1924 the acceptance of the Dawes Plan by Germany's reparation creditors and the stabilization of the German currency made a good impression. Foreign lending expanded and stock flotations dropped in the general slump of 1924. That the latter may have had more influence on the expansion of foreign issues than the Dawes Plan is suggested by the developments of 1925 when the foreign situation improved further. The signing of the Locarno Pacts promised well for peace and many countries reestablished the gold standard, yet foreign issues shrank while those of domestic stocks increased.

In 1926 and through most of 1927 domestic stock issues moved downward and foreign bond issues upward. The latter reached their peak in the first quarter of 1928, half a year after domestic stock issues had begun to turn up.

In the next 5 quarters stock issues increased fourfold while foreign bond issues dropped to one-fourth of their volume. Evidently the striking coincidence of these developments was due to the preference of the American public for speculative shares. The market for new foreign bond issues stumbled under the shock of the speculative boom, though prosperity continued in most countries. The *Handbook on American Underwriting of Foreign Securities* stresses the restrictive influence of American money market conditions upon American underwriting of foreign securities in 1929 (p. 38). But it says also: "adverse political and economic conditions abroad were among the chief causes for the sharp decline" of foreign lending. It refers to the tardiness of the Young Plan negotiations and the decline in the price of some agricultural products. But these are hindsight considerations; actually conditions in 1928 and 1929 seemed prosperous, and it was not skepticism about the situation of the debtor countries but the nationwide speculation in stocks that apparently stopped foreign lending. Indeed, at the very moment in the second half of 1929 when the volume of new domestic stock issues began to fall, foreign issues immediately reappeared.

Thus, except for 1923 and some short lags at the turning points, foreign bond flotations moved counter to domestic common stock issues. Even when the situation abroad was definitely favorable, foreign bond issues declined when domestic stocks expanded, and increased despite unfavorable conditions in the borrowing countries when American stocks made fewer claims on the market.

The question remains why fluctuations in the ratio of expected profits to interest rates should have affected domestic bonds less systematically than foreign bonds. We suggest two possible explanations. First, the higher yields of foreign bonds appeal to the investor who is willing to take greater risks for the sake of larger returns. He is the type of investor who buys common stock also. Consequently, foreign bonds are more sensitive to fluctuations in the stock market than domestic bonds which are more independent, as they are bought in part by a different class of investors. Second, when domestic business improves, investors in general are likely to prefer domestic to foreign securities, and vice versa. This may be another force of considerable importance discouraging foreign flotations during business expansions and stimulating them during contractions; domestic issues are under the opposite influence. In short, foreign bonds are tied closely to domestic business cycles both because they are foreign and because they are bonds.

These tentative conclusions must suffice here. A full analysis still needs to be worked out, especially as to how changes in the character of investor demand are transmitted to foreign issuers. Moreover, it would be well to supplement the analysis of foreign bond cycles by an examination of fluctuations in foreign equity investment. Unfortunately, too few shares of foreign corporations were issued in the United States for reliable conclusions. From 1920 through 1925 there were only 8 offerings. The number increased during the next 4 years, especially in 1928 and 1929, but the total par value for the decade 1920-29 was only $122 million (Table 5). Foreign stock issues declined invariably when foreign bond issues expanded and, in every year except 1929, rose when bond issues dropped. This agrees with our interpretation of foreign bond cycles, but the observations are too few to have much significance.

Table 5

Foreign Common Stock and Foreign Government Bonds Issued in the United States

Year of Issue	Stocks	Bonds	Stocks	Bonds
	($ million)		(year to year change)	
1920	7	439		
1921	0	532	—	+
1922	0	660	0	+
1923	10	303	+	—
1924	0	912	—	+
1925	10	818	+	—
1926	11	673	+	—
1927	9	1,023	—	+
1928	41	875	+	—
1929	34	253	—	—

Bonds: See Table 3.
Stocks: Department of Commerce, *Handbook on American Underwriting of Foreign Securities* (1930), Tables 5 and 7, pp. 15, 17: 'Foreign Corporate Common Stocks' minus 'Common Stock Issues of American and Semi-American Corporations for Non-Domestic Purposes'.

Chapter 2

The Default Index

We turn now to our main topic, fluctuations in the quality of loans. Let us first recall a few well known facts about the history of defaults on foreign bonds. During the entire period of foreign lending, 1920-30, no bond in our record defaulted except two Brazilian state issues. Even on these two, interest payments were maintained until 1929 and 1931 respectively and only the sinking funds were defaulted in 1924 and 1925.[1] The 1920's were the defaultless era in foreign lending. The absence of defaults during such a long period and for about 800 individual investments of this type is remarkable.[2]

Almost all the defaults of the interwar period occurred between 1931 and 1934 under the impact of the great depression. As governmental revenues dwindled with business activity, some governments found that they could not raise the funds for foreign debt service. And even had such funds been available in local currencies their transfer into dollars would have been difficult. Foreign lending had ceased and American imports, the chief remaining source of dollars, shrank in volume and even more in value. Seeing their gold or dollar reserves dwindling many governments attempted to protect their currencies by establishing exchange control and defaulting on their foreign debts. Revolutionary governments — Bolivia, Peru, Chile, Brazil, Cuba, and Germany — especially were inclined to adopt this policy. They "seldom realize fully the

[1] There was a very small number of defaults on bonds not covered by our analysis. The only government issue among these was one of Chinese government notes offered in 1919 and defaulted in 1921; the others were corporate bonds.

[2] Absence of defaults was characteristic of all foreign lending, not just American. ". . . it is true to say that [at the beginning of the depression] the world had been free from any substantial measure of default for more than ten years." *Problem of International Investment,* Royal Institute of International Affairs, 1937, p. 299.

importance of maintaining the credit standing of their country and are more apt to take drastic measures with less regard for the consequences".[3]

The first defaults occurred in Latin America. In January 1931 Bolivia suspended service on its dollar bonds. Peru, Chile, Brazil, Colombia, and Costa Rica followed suit in rapid succession. In 1932 Uruguay and El Salvador, and in 1933 Panama and Cuba, failed to meet their external obligations.

In 1932, one year later than in Latin America, a wave of European defaults set in, which spread rapidly through the agricultural countries of eastern Europe (Hungary, Greece, Bulgaria, Yugoslavia, and Rumania). In Germany the republican government met its foreign obligations despite the acute financial crisis. But when the National Socialist party came into power in 1933 it immediately reduced and soon after suspended payments on dollar bonds. The Dawes and Young loans, which at first were excluded from the moratorium, defaulted one year later. The great wave of defaults was over in 1934 and during the remaining interwar years only one major default occurred, that of Poland in 1936.

Outside Europe and Latin America payments were maintained on practically all dollar loans. The Canadian province of Alberta and a few Canadian municipalities were the exceptions.

Thus the period of the twenties when foreign lending flourished and no foreign loans defaulted was followed in the thirties by a period of defaults in which the market for new foreign issues practically disappeared.

In most cases when defaults on government and government controlled loans occurred, all the loans granted to the country in question were affected simultaneously. The usual procedure was for the government of the defaulting country to prohibit the transfer of debt payments, which meant that all loans owed by the country were in default. Some governments initially exempted certain loans from transfer prohibitions but almost all such exceptions were brief. Hence the only differences between the individual loans of the country in question were short intervals between the

[3] Madden et al., op. cit., p. 120.

dates of their defaults. In some countries where partial service was maintained on defaulted loans, the degree of default differed for different loans, more foreign exchange being allowed for the service of certain loans than for others.

The following countries were exceptions in that they defaulted on some of their issues but maintained payments on others in full: Canada, Argentina, Panama, Cuba, and Czechoslovakia. All other countries, in 1937, were in default on all or none of their bonds.

1 *The Sound Loan Curve*

In examining the changes in the quality of foreign loans our concern is not with the time of their defaulting but with the time of their issue. We want to construct a series of the flotations of defaulted loans and compare it with the series of flotations of all foreign loans described in Chapter 1. Our aim is to determine how the proportion of defaulted loans to total loans varied during our period.

We shall discuss the definition of 'defaulted loan' used in the following investigation at length in Section 2. Here we need merely state that defaulted loans are defined as those granted to a borrower who was in partial or total default on December 31, 1937.

To classify each loan in our record as 'sound' or 'defaulted' we ascertained its fate with the help of the *Annual Reports* of the Foreign Bondholders' Protective Council, the *Bulletins* of the Institute of International Finance, Kimber's *Record of Government Debts,* White, Weld & Co.'s annual publication, *Foreign Dollar Bonds,* and investment manuals. The *Handbook,* our source for the volume of offerings, does not cover defaults, as it was published before their time.

Having determined the status of each issue we split our original series of total bond offerings into two parts: flotations of sound and of defaulted foreign bonds. The varying relation between these two series is the object of our investigation. Before expressing it as a ratio, however, we present the absolute figures of sound loan flotations. Certain facts can be brought out věry clearly by this series (Chart 4).

First, the sound loan curve shows the same distinct 3 cycles and

Chart 4
Sound and Total Foreign Government Bonds Issued in the United States, 1920-1930

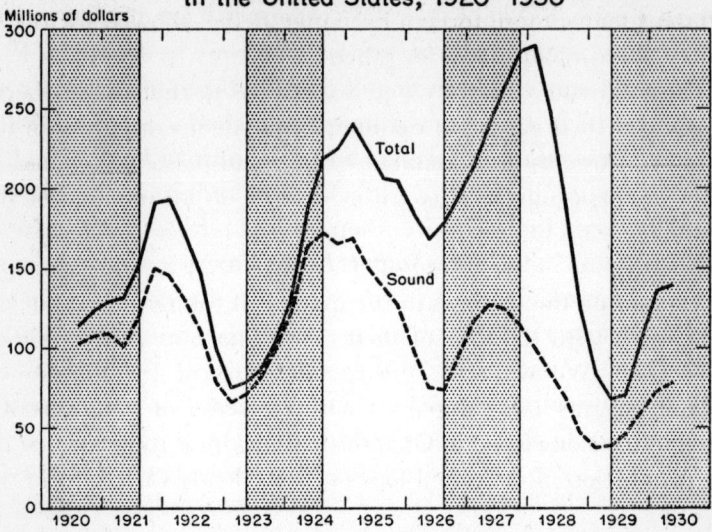

Shaded areas represent contractions, white areas, expansions of business cycles according to NBER chronology. Four quarter moving averages, centered; Appendix Tables 13 and 14.

the same inverse relation to general business cycles as total foreign bond flotations. With a few minor and one major exception every rise and every fall in total loans was accompanied by a simultaneous rise and fall in sound loans. The major exception is a difference in timing: the peaks of the sound loan curve lead the peaks of the total loan curve and this lead lengthens from cycle to cycle until in the last cycle sound loans reach their peak 3 quarters earlier than total loans and decline considerably while total issues are still rising sharply. Lending peaks, evidently, were reached in every case, and especially in the last cycle, in the face of a decline of sound loans. Second, in contrast to the successively rising waves of the total loan curve, the last peak of the sound loan curve is the lowest of the 3. Sound lending was largest in 1924 and in the last cycle declined not only in proportion to the total, as the ratios will show, but even absolutely.

2 Definition of the Default Index

The changing distribution of the flotations of each year among sound and unsound loans is brought out more clearly by percentages. We call the ratio of defaulted loans to all loans issued the 'default index'. When we say the default index of 1926 was 60 percent we mean that of the total amount of loans floated in 1926 60 percent was granted to borrowers who were in default in 1937.

To avoid misunderstanding it should be noted that we use 'default index' in a sense not ordinarily attached to it. At first blush, 'default index' might be taken to mean the ratio of loans defaulting to those outstanding during a period. A default index in this sense would be zero for 1920-30 when no defaults occurred. In the 1930's it would indicate the impact of the different stages of depression on outstanding foreign loans. Our default index, on the contrary, is designed to measure the impact of the changing conditions of the 1920's on the quality of new issues.

Before presenting the default index we discuss the criteria by which we classified a loan as defaulted or not. a) Decisive for the classification of bonds outstanding on December 31, 1937 was their status on that date. We chose this date for the close of the interwar period rather than December 1938 because at the end of 1938 Europe, after the occupation of Austria and Sudetenland, was already under the impact of the forces that came into full power during the war. We decided against a postwar date because of the extraordinary situation still prevailing in a number of countries. However in order to check our findings we examined the default status at the close of 1949 of bonds issued in 1921 and 1928, and find the results substantially confirmed (see below). b) We classified a bond as defaulted when bondholders had not received by December 31, 1937 payments due them according to the original loan contract in full in dollars. Failure to observe the gold clause or payment in Canadian rather than in United States dollars has not been regarded as default.[4] Bonds also were not regarded as defaulted if payments were delayed provided the issuers' obligation was met by December 31, 1937.[5] This applies

[4] In 1937 no gold dollar bonds were being served in gold (in so far as the Council of Foreign Bondholders was informed). Foreign Bondholders Protective Council, *Annual Report, 1938*, p. 24.

[5] With one exception: one issue was classified as 'sound' though its default was not *completely* made up before the end of 1937. In this case the deviation was so slight that it could be disregarded. The bond's price at the end of 1937 was 94.

to a few countries that resumed full service after a short interruption of transfer on foreign debts and paid the arrears.

c) In computing the default index we did not differentiate among degrees of default. It seemed preferable to supplement the default index by a special index of the degree of default (see Sec. 5). The statement "60% of all bonds issued in 1926 went into default" carries a definite meaning, which would be blurred if some bonds were counted, say, as 30 or 60 percent defaulted. Using a rough measure such as the default index seems justified also from the business point of view, which tends to regard any loan in default as a mistake. Besides, payments on defaulted interest coupons represented only a small percentage of the total amount of matured coupons on defaulted bonds. According to Madden et al,[6] of the total amount of matured coupons on bonds defaulted after January 1, 1931 and outstanding at the end of 1935, only 11.8 percent had been paid in cash between January 1931 and December 31, 1935.

d) The most difficult question in rating investments arises from the fact that some loans were partly or totally repaid before the end of our period. At first glance this might seem the clearest case of all. Surely a bond redeemed must be a sound bond and must be classified as such. For purposes of the default index we have, however, decided otherwise. The reason is that, as will be demonstrated below, classification of all repaid loans as sound would bias the results of our analysis in favor of the hypothesis that the proportion of defaulted loans increased during the period under review.

Clearly a loan issued in 1920 will on the average have more chance of being repaid before, say, 1932, than a loan of 1929. Its term may have expired; sinking fund payments may have served to redeem a larger proportion of its original value; finally, the longer a callable bond is outstanding the greater the chance that for some reason the borrower will decide to repay it before maturity. Consequently the percentage of early loans that was repaid and therefore out of danger when the crisis struck was larger than that of later ones.

[6] Op. cit., p. 130.

THE DEFAULT INDEX 35

The resulting downward bias to the default index for the early years is illustrated by the following hypothetical case: Two borrowers, A and B, each issue the same amount of bonds in 1920 and again in 1930. By the depression year 1932, 80 percent of the 1920 bonds but only 20 percent of the 1930 bonds has been repaid. Borrower A defaults in 1932, borrower B remains solvent.

	YEAR OF ISSUE					
	1920			1930		
	BORROWER			BORROWER		
	A	B	A & B	A	B	A & B
Amount issued	100	100	200	100	100	200
Amount repaid before 1932	80	80		20	20	
Amount in default in 1932	20	0	20	80	0	80
1 Default index[a]			$\frac{20}{200} = 10\%$			$\frac{80}{200} = 40\%$
2 Default index[b]			$\frac{20+80}{200} = 50\%$			$\frac{80+20}{200} = 50\%$

[a] All repaid loans counted as 'good'.
[b] Loans repaid by borrowers who subsequently defaulted counted as 'bad' (see text).

When repaid parts of loans count as 'good', the default index for loans issued in 1920 is 10 percent, that for loans issued in 1930, 40 percent. The default index for 1930 rises sharply relative to that for 1920 despite the assumption that the loans granted in both years were alike except for their date of issue. This increase is not meaningless. It does show how much better the outcome of the 1920 investments was than that of the 1930 investments. However, this difference is due solely to the lapse of time between flotation and default.

Actually the role of repayments was not nearly as great as in our example and counting repaid loans as 'good' would only moderately depress the default indexes for the early years.[7] Still, we want to eliminate this factor in order to minimize doubts regarding the validity of our results. We have, therefore, devised the following treatment of loans fully or partly repaid. We distinguish between two types of such loans. First, loans that were partly or fully repaid by borrowers who did not default on any of their debts

[7] See Appendix Table 19.

in the 1930's are counted as sound. There is no good reason why a loan whose issuer remained solvent in the 1930's should be considered as unsound. One might object that early repayments of parts of its foreign debt may have enabled a country to maintain payments on the remainder during the crisis, thus preventing defaults that would otherwise have occurred. This may be granted; yet a debt policy that eased a country's position in the depression and enabled it to avoid bankruptcy is certainly no justification for classifying that country's issues as unsound. Second, partly or fully repaid loans by borrowers who defaulted on any issue are counted as defaulted on the assumption that in this case repayment was due to the fact that the loan was granted early in the period.

Using this method in the above example we obtain the same default index for loans issued in 1920 as for those issued in 1930. This agrees with our assumption that the two pairs of loans were alike except for their date of issue. This treatment of repaid loans obviously affords a most rigorous test for the hypothesis that defaulted loans constituted a rising proportion of all loans issued. Counting loans of earlier years as unsound when in themselves they were sound and did not bring the investor a loss, imparts a declining bias to the trend of the default index. If the index still shows a rising trend, as it does, we can be confident that this cannot be due to our method of computation.

The problem of repaid loans cannot, of course, be solved by excluding them entirely from the investigation and dealing only with loans outstanding at a given time. A measure of the quality of the lending of a period must comprise all loans issued during this period. The meaninglessness of a measure relating only to loans outstanding at a certain time becomes evident if we assume, e.g., that 99 of the 100 issues of a period were repaid before the crisis and that the single remaining issue defaulted. The default index would be 100 percent, clearly an unacceptable measure of loan quality.[8] If the interval between the time of issue and the date

---

[8] Applying our method, the 99 repaid issues would be divided into 2 groups: those repaid by borrowers who did and those repaid by borrowers who did not default later on. If, say, 9 of the 99 repaid issues belonged in the latter group, the default index would be 10 percent.

THE DEFAULT INDEX 37

when the outstanding loans are examined is sufficiently long, a default index derived in this way would always approach 100 percent, since all except the defaulted loans would have been repaid.

3 Description of the Default Index

Two default indexes are presented in Chart 5. Default index A is for foreign loans in the wider sense, i.e., it includes Canadian issues; default index B is for foreign issues exclusive of Canadian loans. The steep upsweep of both curves shows that the quality of new foreign issues declined sharply during the 1920's. We note further that, like business in general, the default index rises in 3

Chart 5
Default Index: Foreign Government Bonds Issued in the United States, 1920-1930

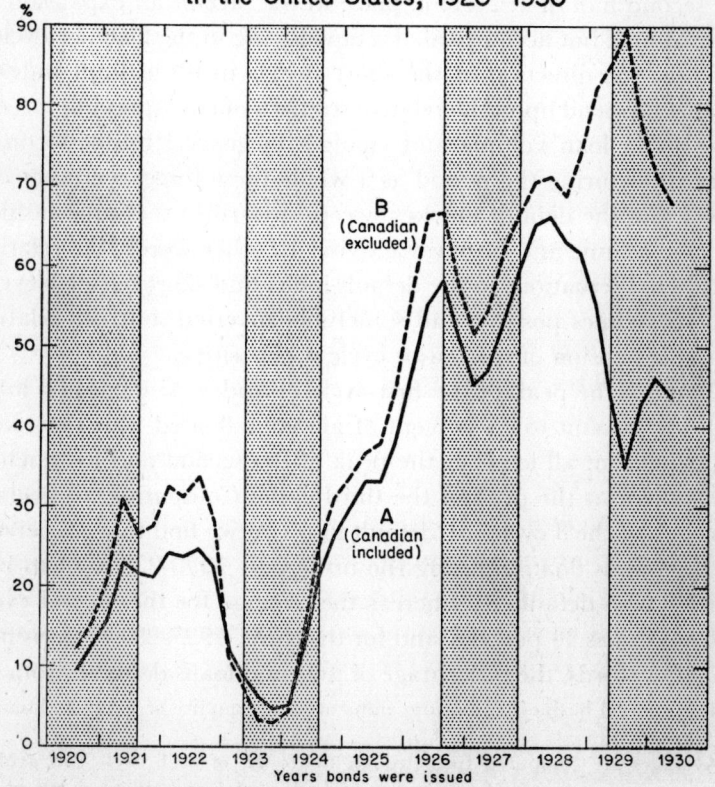

Shaded areas represent contractions, white areas, expansions of business cycles according to NBER chronology. Four quarter moving averages, centered; Appendix Table 14.

successive waves. But the timing of these waves differs from that of the 3 business cycles; foreign loan quality moved sometimes parallel with and at other times counter to cycles in general business. This instability may be due to the inverse relation between fluctuations in foreign loan issues and business cycles. For part of the period, approximately until the end of 1924 and in 1927, the proportion of defaulted loans rose and fell with the amount of lending, so that there was an inverse relation between the default index and business cycles. But between the first quarter of 1925 and the second quarter of 1926 the default index rose steeply with the expansion in business activity and despite the decline in new issues (default index A from 30 to 55 percent; default index B from 34 to 66 percent). And the improvement of loan quality in the second half of 1926 took place in the face of an expansion in loan volume but accompanied a downswing in the business cycle.[9]

Thus, the direction of the short swings in the default indexes seems to depend upon the relative strength of two opposing forces: changes in loan volume and changes in general business conditions. But during the period as a whole these forces were not opposed and the default indexes sweep upward in the same fashion as loan volume and business activity. In other words, the relation between fluctuations in the default index and short business cycles was sometimes positive and sometimes inverted, but the relation to the expansion of the major cycle was positive.

Even at the peak of the first cycle of 'index A' defaulted loans did not amount to 25 percent of all loans floated. But they were 58 percent of all loans at the peak of the second and as much as 66 percent at the peak of the third cycle. Computing an average for each of the 3 cycles in 'default index A' we find that 19 percent of the bonds floated during the first cycle, 1920-23, went to borrowers who defaulted; whereas the average for the second cycle, 1923-27, was 34 percent, and for the third, 1927-29, 57 percent.[10] In other words, the percentage of unsound loans doubled from the

[9] How general business conditions influenced the quality of loans is discussed in Chapter 6.

[10] Averages are computed from trough to trough of each cycle. To avoid a downward bias due to the inclusion of both initial and terminal troughs in computing the cyclical average, the trough values are weighted one-half each.

THE DEFAULT INDEX

first to the second cycle and tripled from the first to the third. The quality of credit declined steeply.

When Canadian loans are excluded, results are even more striking. Since few Canadian loans defaulted, index B is considerably higher than A. The higher level does not, of course, imply anything about the slope of the series which, however, was even steeper than that of index A (Chart 5). Index B increases from 34 percent at its first peak to 67 at the second and to 90 at the third. The 3 cycle averages are 24, 40, and 68 percent. Evidently Canadian loans were a stabilizing element as far as loan quality was concerned.[11]

[11] The default index by geographic groups of borrowing countries is analyzed in Chapter 3.

Chart 6
Default Index Based on Number of Issues
Foreign Government Bonds Issued in the United States
1920 – 1930

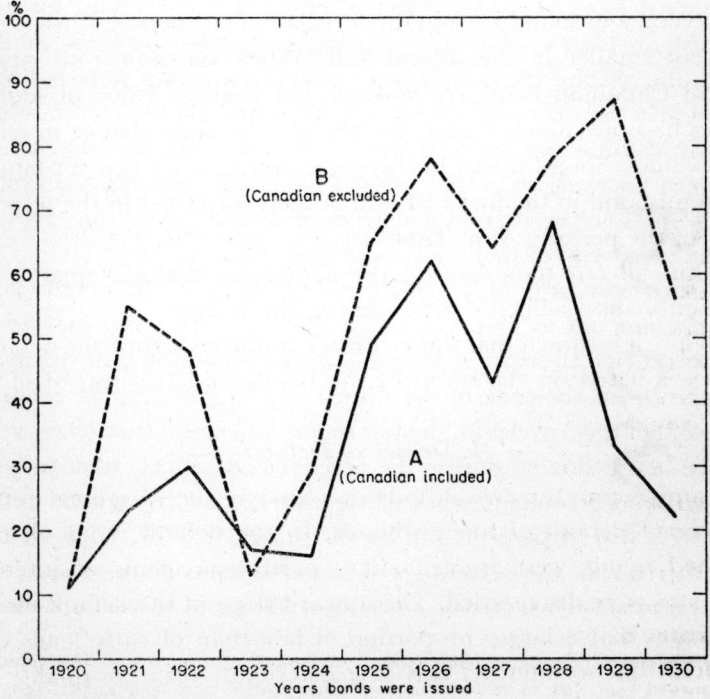

Appendix Table 15.

To increase confidence in our results we test them further by computing a default index in terms of the number of bond issues instead of their dollar value. Because of the big variations in the amounts of individual issues ($10,000 to $125,000,000), the number of issues is a poor measure of lending. We use it solely to test the stability of our results. As we are interested mainly in the broad movements of the indexes, we simplify the procedure by using annual data on the number of issues instead of moving averages of quarterly data (Chart 6). These curves too tend strongly upward, supporting the previous results. Default indexes A and B both roughly double whether we compare the first and the last peak or the averages for the first and last cycle. The slopes are less steep than those of the default index for the dollar amount of loans, indicating that the deterioration of credit involved a change in the relative size of sound and unsound loans as well as in their number. While the average sound issue was 3 percent larger than the average unsound issue in the first half of the period, it was $2\frac{1}{2}$ percent smaller in the second half. When the numerous small sound Canadian loans are omitted, the average value of sound issues becomes much higher. Yet there is the same change in relative values. Sound loans, in this case, averaged 85 percent larger than unsound in the first half and 59 percent larger in the second half of the period (App. Table 16).

Thus all our tests confirm the hypothesis that the quality of foreign loans declined sharply during the 1920's.

Below it is shown that this is further confirmed when the default index is based on the status of the bonds in 1949 instead of in 1937.

4 *Degree of Default*

To supplement the default index we analyze the variations in the degree of default of foreign bonds. In the default index all defaulted bonds were treated alike; partial payments of interest coupons were disregarded. The upward slope of the default index indicates that a larger proportion of late than of early loans defaulted. But to interpret this as a deterioration in the quality of loans we must assume that the degree of default remained constant

THE DEFAULT INDEX 41

over the period. Conceivably loans issued in early years might have defaulted completely and those of later years kept up a partial service. In this way the rise in the default index might be offset by a decline in the degree of default. Was there such an offsetting improvement in defaulted loans? If defaulted loans floated in the later years were no better than those floated in the earlier years, our interpretation of the default index is justified.

Differences among defaulted bonds are reflected to some extent in their prices. The average price on December 31, 1937 of the defaulted bonds issued, say, in 1925, may serve as an index of the degree of their default. A series of such indexes by the date of issue of the bonds measures the variations in the degree of default. Accordingly, we computed the arithmetic mean of the prices of defaulted bonds issued at a given time, weighted by the par values of the issues.[12] Not all bonds counted as defaulted in the default index are contained in the price index. Repaid loans, obviously, had to be omitted. A few minor issues in foreign currencies also had to be excluded because a price in dollars could not be ascertained. The price index comprises 81 percent of the number and 91 percent of the dollar value of the bonds in the default index.

Chart 7 shows that there was no change in the degree of default that would offset the change in the default index.[13] Average prices at the close of 1937 of bonds issued in 1927 and 1928 were about the same as those of bonds issued in 1921 and 1922, namely 20-25 percent of their par value.

The price of a bond does not by any means, of course, reflect merely the degree of its default. It depends also upon expectations of the market and on policies pursued by the debtors. To evaluate the price index correctly, we must therefore note some of the special factors affecting bond prices in 1937. Prices of German bonds, which constitute a large part of the unsound bonds issued in the late twenties, were much higher in 1937 than the payments

---

[12] 4 quarter moving averages of weighted prices are divided by 4 quarter moving averages of weights.

[13] This curve cannot be interpreted like an ordinary price index. It does *not* reflect changes in a group of prices over time. It shows prices quoted on one date for bonds floated at different times.

Chart 7
**Average Price on December 31, 1937
of Defaulted Foreign Government Bonds Issued
in the United States, by Time of Issue, 1920–1930**

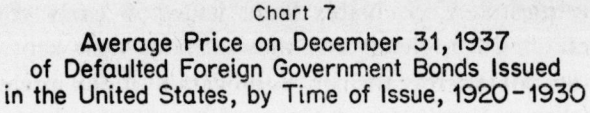

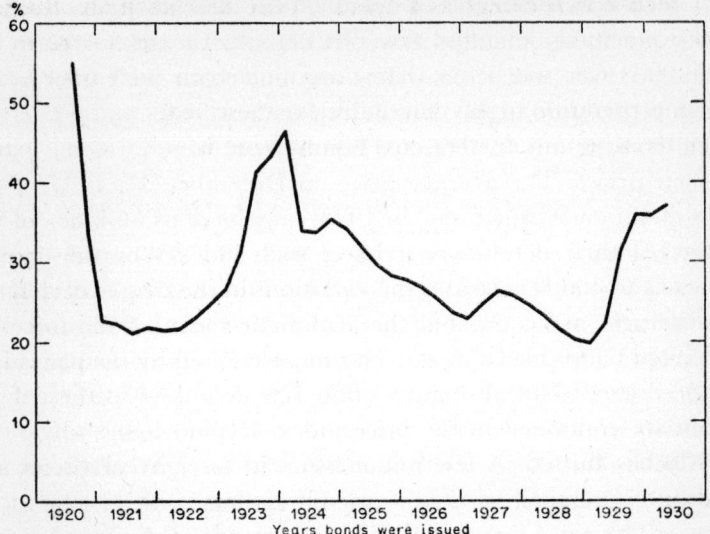

Four quarter moving averages, centered; Appendix Table 14.

their holders received could have explained. After prolonged delay the German authorities finally, in March 1937, issued 3 percent funding bonds in lieu of interest payments due on nonReich German bonds since June 1934. But even these funding bonds were available only for coupons matured before the end of 1936; no provision whatever was made for coupons maturing later. Yet these bonds were quoted at about 20 because confidence in Germany was still relatively high and because Germany herself was in the market to buy her own defaulted bonds, thus raising their prices. Quotations for Latin American defaulted bonds were relatively much lower. For instance, Brazilian bonds, which constitute a large part of the unsound bonds issued in the early twenties, brought about the same prices as the German though they paid in 1937 from 32½ to 50 percent of interest due. This relative overvaluation of part of the defaulted loans of later years imparts an upward bias to the price index. If the index still does not show a rising tendency, we can be satisfied that defaulted loans of the late twenties were no better than defaulted loans of the early twenties.

We do not attribute much significance to the price index of defaulted bonds except as a check on the default index. Such an index inevitably includes few observations at times when — as in 1920, 1921, and 1923 — few unsound loans were issued. The index is therefore highly unreliable for these years and we refrain from drawing any further conclusions from it.

5 *Note on the Present Status of Foreign Bonds*

What has happened to foreign bonds since 1937? Were they greatly affected by the World War? Did the world shaking events of the last decade make the bad debtors solvent and the good ones bankrupt? The answer is no. The great majority of countries that serviced their loans in full in 1937 did so in 1949; most of the countries in default in 1937 were in default in 1949.

What is the explanation of this consistency? Were the economies of countries in default worse off during these 12 years than those of solvent countries? For many countries this cannot be the explanation. Half of the defaulted loans were issued by Latin American countries that were highly prosperous during the war with booming dollar exports. Many good issues, on the other hand, were from countries that were invaded and occupied and suffered grievously. Belgium, France, and Norway, for example, kept paying all they owed; others, such as Peru and Bolivia, paid and pay almost nothing. Though most South American countries did improve service on their loans not one of those in default in 1937 decided to pay its creditors their due.[14]

In view of these facts no revolutionary changes in the default index are to be expected when the status of the bonds on December 31, 1949 instead of December 31, 1937 is used to classify them. To give some idea of the magnitude and direction of these changes we recomputed the default index for 2 years, each fairly represen-

[14] Argentine bonds, except a few provincial issues, were not in default in 1937. A few Central American and Caribbean countries in partial default in 1937 have completely repaired their defaults, e.g., Cuba, Dominican Republic, Guatemala.

tative for its period, 1921 and 1928. The increase in the proportion of defaulted issues again stands out clearly. Canadian loans are included. Default is defined as before: any deviation from contractual payments. Defaulted loans are loans to borrowers in default at the close of 1949.

The new default index for issues of 1921 is 44 percent, that for issues of 1928 74 percent. The corresponding figures based on the default status of 1937 are 34 percent for 1921 and 68 percent for 1928. The difference between the two pairs of indexes is due almost entirely to Danish issues, which were not in default in 1937. In 1949 Denmark was paying interest fully as stipulated, but had not yet resumed full service on sinking funds or repaid an issue due in 1942. The latter, however, was quoted at 94 at the close of 1949. Except for Danish issues the two indexes based on 1949 would differ only fractionally from the corresponding ones based on 1937. The few changes that did occur during these 12 eventful years roughly offset one another.

During the long period since foreign bonds first defaulted debtors have made various arrangements with their creditors, arrangements that fulfill contractual obligations more or less completely. In other words partial default now plays a greater role than in 1937. In several countries old bonds have been exchanged for new ones with lower interest rates, and it is sometimes a matter of opinion whether the original issue is still to be counted among defaulted issues. To indicate how decisions about the doubtful cases affect the default index, we make the experiment of shifting defaulted issues quoted at 75 or higher at the close of 1949 to sound issues. The results are not altered materially. The new index for 1921 is 31 percent, that for 1928, 63 percent; both standings are remarkably similar to those based on the default status in 1937.

Measured against the events in these 12 years the change in the default status of debtor countries was certainly slight. The resulting stability of the default index enhances its significance as a measure of loan quality. The unchanging character of nations as debtors has further interesting implications for the interpretation of defaults and loan deterioration (see Ch. 6).

6 *In Conclusion*

The statistical investigation has established as a fact what was before surmised by some,[15] denied by others, and ignored by the majority of economists: that the quality of foreign bond issues changed materially during the nineteen twenties. The 'lending of the twenties', as far as time of lending is concerned, has usually been treated as one homogeneous mass to all parts of which much the same explanation is appropriate. This simplification may for certain purposes be justified. For others it distorts the picture. In any case general statements about the lending of the twenties are founded upon an average representing very different conditions.

We have applied statistical methods to a subject that seemed unpromising. The foreign lending of the twenties is commonly described as 'erratic' and 'chaotic' and indeed it was subject to strong forces of diverse and varying power. To make the rule of order in this field seem rather unlikely, it suffices to cite events such as the occupation of the Ruhr, the Locarno Pacts, the collapse of European currencies, the reestablishment of the gold standard. Moreover, we are dealing with errors in individual investment judgment which, even apart from the special field of foreign lending, seem too elusive and subjective to possess much order or regularity. It is noteworthy, therefore, that despite the small scope of our investigation, empirical analysis has enabled us to uncover a rational picture and a high degree of order where chaos was supposed to rule.

7 *Note on Two Investigations of Investment Quality*

Two other investigations of investment quality by date of investing substantiate the results of the foreign bond analysis.

One is a study of domestic bonds made by George W. Edwards

---

[15] See particularly an article by Max Winkler in the New York Tribune of March 17, 1927: "Any one who has followed closely the various foreign offerings in this country within recent months could not help noticing the steady decline in the quality of such new loans." Quoted in Max Winkler, *Foreign Bonds, an Autopsy* (Roland Swain, 1933), p. 85.

Cf. also W. A. Brown, op. cit., p. 585, who in discussing American foreign lending remarks on "the appearance of progressively poorer credit risks among the borrowers...."

Table 6

Default Status of Domestic Bonds Outstanding in December 1931, by Date of Issue

Date of Issue	Total No. of Bonds Issued	% of Bonds Defaulting
Before 1900	70	14.3
1900-13	419	14.5
1914-19	206	10.1
1920-22	263	18.6
1923-24	637	18.4
1925-26	371	21.6
1927-28	1,118	31.8
1929	267	31.1
1930-31	496	11.9
No information	551	22.0
Total	4,398	20.2

George W. Edwards, Control of the Security-Investment System, *Harvard Business Review*, Oct. 1933, p. 7.

in 1932. Edwards grouped all 4,398 issues in Fitch's Bond Record in December 1931 by their date of issue and computed the "per cent of the total number issued for each year which were in actual or pending default" in December 1931 (Table 6). "From this table it is seen that of the bonds issued in 1927, 1928, and 1929, 31.1 percent went into actual or pending default, as compared with a much lower percentage for the bonds issued in previous years."[16] Edwards attributes the decline in quality to "conditions of overcompetition and irresponsibility" in which "the purchasing function of investment banking was poorly performed" and "Capital was frequently raised for corporations and for governments whose financial position did not warrant such financial assistance".[17]

Investment of a very different character is the subject of R. J. Saulnier's recent interesting analysis, *Urban Mortgage Lending by*

---

[16] *Harvard Business Review*, Oct. 1933, pp. 6, 7. Edwards' figures refer only to bonds still outstanding in December 1931. If bonds repaid before that date were included the percentage of bonds issued in earlier years and defaulting would be even lower, and the rise of this percentage over the period steeper.

[17] George W. Edwards, *The Evolution of Finance Capitalism* (Longmans, Green, 1938), p. 231.

Life Insurance Companies.[18] "The rapid increase in loan delinquency, which began in the early thirties, soon transformed large segments of the urban mortgage holdings of life insurance companies into owned real estate. But not all types of loans were foreclosed with the same relative frequency, and it is pertinent to inquire which groups of loans had the best, and which the worst, records in this respect. To give quantitative expression to these differences in loan experience, the sample of urban mortgage loans was classified according to relevant characteristics of the loan contracts and of the properties securing them and ratios of the number and original amount of foreclosed loans to the total number and amount of loans, referred to as foreclosure rates, were calculated for several classifications."

Among the many characteristics analyzed for their effect on foreclosure rates is the time of loan origination. Saulnier too found that experience with loans of the twenties differs according to the time of lending. The foreclosure rate for loans made in 1920-24 and not extinguished by the end of 1934 was 24 percent; the corresponding rate for loans made in 1925-29 was 41 percent.[19]

Since these mortgage loans had on the average much shorter terms than the foreign bonds, foreclosure rates are more affected by the exclusion of extinguished loans than our default index. "While the average contract life for all loans made between 1920 and 1934, and extinguished by 1946, was 6.7 years, the defaulted loans had an actual life of 13.9 years between origination and final sale of property, while other loans had an average actual life of 8.3 years."[20] Consequently, most of the sound loans made in 1920-24 had been extinguished by 1935, 10 to 15 years after they were made, while a much larger proportion of defaulted loans had not yet been disposed of. This must be taken into account if the foreclosure rate for this period, 24 percent, is to be evaluated correctly. A large part of the sound loans made during the next 5 years, on the contrary, did not expire until after 1934. This, of course, tends to pull down the foreclosure rate for loans made in

[18] National Bureau of Economic Research, 1950, p. 82.
[19] Based on ibid., Tables 22 and B10.
[20] Ibid., pp. 47-8.

Table 7

Foreclosure Rates on a Sample of Urban Mortgage Loans Made by Life Insurance Companies

PERIOD MADE	1920-24	1925-29	1930-34	1935-39	1940-46	TOTAL OR AVERAGE
NUMBER OF LOANS MADE AND EXTINGUISHED
1920-24	104	503	140	103	83	933
1925-29		254	593	631	606	2,084
1930-34			116	335	316	767
ORIGINAL AMOUNT OF LOANS MADE AND EXTINGUISHED (millions of dollars)
1920-24	.85	4.86	.73	1.16	1.08	8.67
1925-29		2.75	4.68	5.75	10.42	23.61
1930-34			.90	2.12	3.18	6.20
FORECLOSURE RATE
Percentage of Number
1920-24	0	0	4.3	24.3	30.1	6.0
1925-29		.4*	6.7*	32.8*	38.4*	23.1*
1930-34			4.3	21.8	21.2	18.9
Percentage of Amount
1920-24	0	0	3.2	31.5	31.5	8.4
1925-29		.3*	5.7*	40.1*	54.1*	34.8*
1930-34			4.7	25.2	18.3	18.7

* Foreclosure rates on loans made in 1925-29 higher than on those made in the preceding or following quinquennium.

R. J. Saulnier, *Urban Mortgage Lending by Life Insurance Companies* (NBER, 1950), Table B10, family dwellings and all other property combined.

1925-29. Under these circumstances 41 percent must be considered a very high rate.

Moreover, the contrast between the good and the really bad years is smoothed when comparisons are made by 5-year intervals. For instance, the foreclosure rate for the earlier period is pushed up considerably by the inclusion of 1924, which had a much higher foreclosure rate than the preceding years, whereas the rate for the later period is held down by the rate for 1925, which was much lower than the following ones.

Table 7 compares the issues of 1925-29 not only with the preceding but also with the following period. Among the loans extinguished in any given period those made in 1925-29 always had considerably higher foreclosure rates, whether number or amount is the criterion, than those made before or after this time.

Other aspects of mortgage lending brought out by Saulnier's

THE DEFAULT INDEX

investigation reflect "the optimism characteristic of both parties to the mortgage contract at precisely the time when increased caution was warranted"[21] and point to a decline in credit quality in mortgage lending similar to though perhaps less far-reaching than that in foreign lending. Interest rates were lower in 1925-29 than in 1920-24; the relative numbers of the two safest types of loans, those under $5,000 and those fully amortized, were smaller in the later quinquennium. The average size of loans on family dwellings rose 23 percent from 1920-24 to 1925-29; loans on income-producing properties, which had higher foreclosure rates, increased nearly 50 percent in average amount. Moreover, larger loans reflected not only the rise in real estate prices but also an increase in the average ratio of the amount loaned to the value of the property.[22]

All this is interesting for the foreign bond analysis because mortgage loans and domestic bonds are utterly unaffected by anything peculiar to foreign lending, such as transfer troubles or the inexperience of creditors. The three types of investment have only this in common: they originated in the same market and responded similarly to its changing climate. Analysis of investment experience in other fields, e.g., business failures by the time of the establishment of the firm, might reveal a similar change in quality.

[21] Ibid., p. 100.
[22] Ibid., Tables 10 and B3.

Chapter 3

GEOGRAPHIC SHIFTS IN FOREIGN LOANS

Classification of foreign loans by the geographic location of debtor countries tests the diffusion of the process of credit deterioration and helps to interpret it. We now examine changes in the quality of foreign loans in geographic groups of debtor countries and shifts of foreign loans between such groups. Variations in the general default index are viewed as the resultants of these changes and shifts.

Only a minor part of the variation in the default index can be attributed to changes in loan quality within individual borrowing countries. This does not mean that loans issued at different times by public authorities in any particular country were equally sound. On the contrary, in several cases the first loans granted to a country appear to have been cautious and well secured, but were followed by ill advised credits. With few exceptions, however, either all of the foreign loans of the governments in a country went into default or none. Thus, differences that may have existed between loans of the same country disappeared. Only in the few countries where some loans were defaulted while the obligations on others were met may changes in quality be ascertained. These 'mixed' countries are Argentina, Cuba, and Panama (Table 8).[1] Each of the three series of default indexes rises sharply during the later years. This small sample too substantiates our previous results.

The defaulted loans of Argentina, Cuba, and Panama, constituting only about 5 percent of all the defaulted loans in our record, are too insignificant to account materially for the variations in the aggregate default index. The greater part of these variations was not due to changes within but to shifts between individual borrowing countries; or rather, as a glance at the location of 'good' and 'bad' countries will show, to shifts between major geographic areas. 'Good' and 'bad' debtor countries, far from being

[1] Also Canada, which will be discussed below among the larger geographic areas. Outside these countries only one defaulted loan was issued by a public authority in a country that otherwise did not default: a small issue ($1.5 million) by the City of Carlsbad, Czechoslovakia.

Table 8
Annual Default Index: Argentina, Cuba, Panama
(percentages)

	Argentina	Cuba	Panama
1920	....	....	....
1921	0	....	....
1922	0	0	....
1923	....	0	0
1924	0	....	....
1925	18	....	....
1926	56	....	0
1927	22	0	33
1928	47	100	100
1929	....	100	0

distributed evenly over the map of the world, form large clusters; the 'bad' debtors are in Latin America and in central and eastern Europe (referred to hereafter as 'eastern Europe'); 'good' borrowers in northern and western Europe (referred to hereafter as 'western Europe'), the Far East, and Canada. In this grouping 'eastern Europe' is made up of Germany, Danzig, Estonia, Poland, Czechoslovakia, Austria, Hungary, Yugoslavia, Greece, Bulgaria, and Rumania; 'western Europe' of Great Britain, Ireland, France, Italy, Switzerland, Belgium, the Netherlands, Scandinavia, and Finland. Far Eastern debtor countries include Australia, the Netherlands Indies, Japan, and Palestine.

Table 9 shows the great difference between the two 'bad' and the three 'good' areas with respect to the quality of their loans. It also shows the changes that occurred within these groups over the period. The countries of 'western Europe' and the Far East remained entirely free from default. Canada is an exception; its default index was higher for the early period (4.7 percent) than for the later period (3.5 percent). But Canadian defaults were few. The default indexes for the 'bad' areas varied more. The default index for eastern Europe rose from 75 percent in the early

Table 9
Default Index, 5 Geographic Areas

	Western Europe	Far East	Canada	Eastern Europe	Latin America	Total
1920-24	0.0	0.0	4.7	74.8	55.2	17.5
1925-29	0.0	0.0	3.5	91.9	79.4	49.5

to 92 percent in the late period; that for Latin America from 55 to 79 percent. The upward movement of the general default index is repeated in both these subdivisions.

But the change in loan quality within the 5 areas accounts for only a minor part of the total decline. If the share of each of the 5 areas in total borrowing had remained in 1925-29 what it was in 1920-24, the change within the areas would have raised the default index for all loans only from 18 percent for the early to 23 percent for the late period. The difference between 23 percent and the actual rate, 50 percent, is due to shifts in the proportion of loans taken by different areas.

As Table 10 shows, both 'bad areas' took a much larger part of total lending in the late than in the early period, whereas the share of each of the three 'good areas' declined. It is noteworthy that the latter (western Europe, Far East, and Canada) borrowed not only relatively but even absolutely less from the United States in the later period, despite the boom in American foreign lending.

Table 10

Distribution by Geographic Areas
Foreign Government Bonds Issued in the United States

	AMOUNT ($ mil.)		PERCENTAGE SHARE	
	1920-24	1925-29	1920-24	1925-29
Western Europe	1,073	620	37.7	17.3
Far East	343	284	12.1	7.9
Canada	669	617	23.5	17.2
Eastern Europe	233	912	8.1	25.4
Latin America	529	1,158	18.6	32.2
Total	2,847	3,591	100.0	100.0

In sum, the rise in the general default index may be viewed as the result both of the decline in loan quality within 'bad' debtor areas and of shifts of lending from 'good' to 'bad' areas. This diffusion of the process of credit deterioration is an important factor in its evaluation and interpretation. If, for example, the rise in the default index was due solely to mistaken judgment about a single country, this would, of course, have a different meaning from the actual case where loans to many countries that subsequently defaulted increased *and* loans to areas that remained solvent declined.

Chart 8
Foreign Government Bonds Issued in the United States, by Geographic Areas, 1920-24 and 1925-29

[Chart showing Sound Issues and Unsound Issues in billions of dollars, with categories: Canada, Far East, West and North Europe, East and Central Europe, Latin America]

Appendix Table 17.

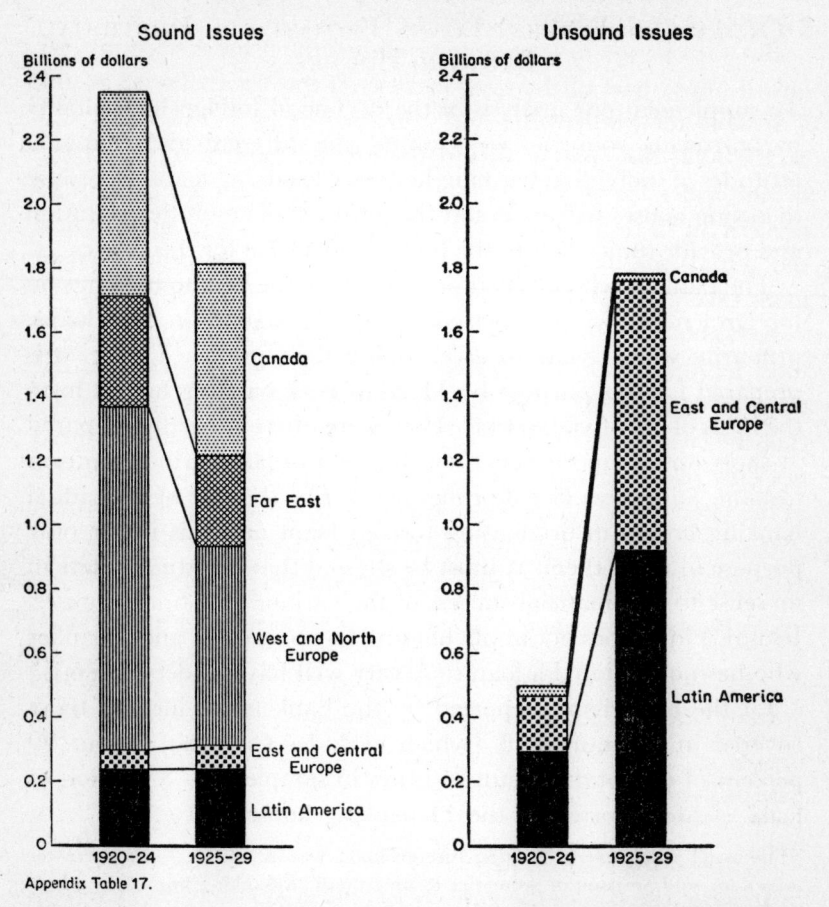

Chart 8 portrays the changes both within and between areas. It is noteworthy that the unsound loans issued in 1925-29 were about evenly distributed between Europe and Latin America. The increase in both these groups of unsound loans and the relative, and in the three major groups even absolute, decline in each subdivision of sound loans, also stand out clearly.[2]

[2] Annual data summarized in Chart 8 and presented in detail in Appendix Table 17 show that the contrast between the two periods is not due to the loans of any single year but reflects a continuous process.

Chapter 4
QUALITY OF FOREIGN LOANS INITIATED BY INDIVIDUAL BANKING HOUSES

To supplement our analysis of the decline in foreign loan quality by borrowing countries we examine the different and changing attitudes of individual banking houses. Classifying loans according to issuing houses will again test the diffusion of credit deterioration and provide some clues to the forces responsible for this process.

The bankers who testified in 1931-32 at the Senate hearings on foreign lending were requested to file information on their loans, primarily with a view to ascertaining their profits. The records prepared for this purpose by 11 New York banking houses form the basis of our investigation. They were often hurriedly prepared at short notice; moreover, they were not organized in a uniform fashion. Still, these lists do roughly describe the role of individual banking houses in originating foreign loans and this is our only purpose in using them. It must be stressed that our study refers in no sense to the financial success of the various investment houses. Issuing a loan does not imply holding any part of it; and a banker who has not initiated a loan may very well have underwritten it.[1]

Of the bond issues reported by the bankers we include those covered in our sample B (which excludes Canada). About 90 percent of the total amount of issues in sample B — $5 billion of loans — are reported by the 11 banking houses.

---

[1] The usual procedure in floating foreign loans was as follows: The borrower as vendor sold an issue of securities to an American banking house, the originating or issuing house. The originating house either marketed the entire issue itself, or, more commonly, associated itself with one or several other investment houses, forming a buying or underwriting syndicate. The participants in such a syndicate "do not actually purchase the securities, but instead underwrite them. That is, they guarantee or really insure the sale of an issue by agreeing to an arrangement whereby the unsold balance of an issue is taken over" (G. W. Edwards, *Investing in Foreign Securities,* Ronald Press, 1926, pp. 110-1).

The original house usually managed the syndicate it had organized. The underwriting syndicate disposed of the securities to the distributing syndicate, a large association including possibly hundreds of participants, which in turn offered the bonds to the public.

LOANS BY INDIVIDUAL BANKING HOUSES 55

The statistical data presented in this chapter are not as trustworthy as those presented in earlier chapters. They are based on less reliable compilations, as indicated above, and they do not cover all issuing houses. Furthermore, the lending of each banking house is, of course, only a fraction of total lending, and as the number of observations becomes smaller, measurements are more affected by special factors which tended to cancel out when all loans were treated as a whole. Thus the findings of this chapter must be taken as rough approximations. Yet for all their limitations the results are surprisingly stable and the story they tell seems so reasonable that they are well worth studying.[2]

Arraying the 11 investment houses in the order of the soundness of the loans they originated we get the results shown in Table 11 (for definitions of 'sound' and 'defaulted' loans see Ch. 2). The differences in the activity and judgment of individual banking houses are striking. The wide range of the default indexes is the more remarkable as the "responsible and prudent issuing houses . . . are liable to be blacklegged in negotiating their business and

[2] As an experiment we added first Canadian, then private corporate loans to our sample. The results were essentially the same as those shown below.

Table 11

Default Index, 11 Banking Houses, 1920-1930

BANKING HOUSE	AMOUNT OF FOREIGN GOVERNMENT LOANS INITIATED All ($ million)	Defaulted ($ million)	DEFAULT INDEX (%)
1	323	43	13
2	1,680	232	14
3	377	100	27
4	314	103	33
5	832	397	48
6	468	338	72
7	157	126	80
8	233	227	97
9	294	284	97
10	133	131	98
11	157	157	100
A Group (1-2)	2,003	275	14
B Group (3-5)	1,523	600	39
C Group (6-11)	1,442	1,263	88
Total	4,968	2,138	43

to have sound transactions made unsound by subsequent extravagance".[3] When the banking houses are grouped by their default indexes it turns out that Group A, the initiators of $2 billions of loans, assessed risks so well that only 14 percent of their issues went to borrowers who defaulted; but more than one-third of the issues of Group B, which initiated $1.5 billion of loans, and almost nine-tenths of the nearly $1.5 billion initiated by Group C proved unsound. To put it differently: only 13 percent of defaulted loans stemmed from bankers who originated 40 percent of all loans, while 59 percent stemmed from bankers who issued only 29 percent of all loans.

Though equality was not to be expected in view of the different characters of investment houses and the role of chance, the range of default indexes for individual banking houses, 13-100 percent, is astonishing. Evidently the factors determining the quality of credit were not of uniform importance for all bankers. Some issuing houses must have been almost immune to the forces which caused the deterioration of credit. Others, on the contrary, were utterly under their sway.

Are the differences between banking houses due to the different timing of their loans? That is, did those with a low default index extend loans primarily in the early period, and those with a high default index in the late period? Or does a low default index mean that a banking house lent wisely throughout the period and a high one that it made serious mistakes all the time?

Table 12 reveals that the decline in loan quality was widely diffused. The default index of only 1 of the 11 banking houses did not decline. This makes the rise in the general default index more meaningful and strongly supports our interpretation of it as a gauge of credit deterioration.

The timing of the loans and their outcome were closely related. The more the lending of a banking house was concentrated in the second half of the period the more unfavorable the result (col. 3 and 4).[4] Of the four most careful lenders two lent less after

[3] Salter, op. cit., p. 123.
[4] The coefficient of rank correlation between the degree to which loans were concentrated in the second period (col. 3) and the default index (col. 4) is .92.

Table 12
Timing and Quality of Foreign Government Bond Issues Initiated by 11 Banking Houses

	AMOUNT OF LOANS INITIATED ($ million)		RATIO: Loans 1925-30 to Loans 1920-30	DEFAULT INDEX (percentages)		
BANKING HOUSE	1920-24	1925-30		1920-30	1920-24	1925-30
	(1)	(2)	(3)	(4)	(5)	(6)
1	150	173	54	13	0	25
2	869	811	48	14	15	12
3	213	164	44	27	0	61
4	147	167	53	33	0	62
5	311	521	63	48	8	71
6	188	280	60	72	57	82
7	37	120	76	80	62	86
8	39	194	83	97	85	100
9	6	288	98	97	....*	99
10	0	133	100	98	....	98
11	0	157	100	100	....	100
A Group (1-2)	1,019	984	49	14	13	14
B Group (3-5)	671	852	56	39	4	67
C Group (6-11)	270	1,172	81	88	61	94
Total	1,960	3,008	61	43	17	60

* This firm did not issue a loan until 1926 except for a single issue in 1920. In this case, it would be pointless to speak of a default index of zero for 1920-24. Therefore we disregard this loan here and in the discussion of the default indexes for 1920-24.

1924 than before; the other two lent only slightly more. At the other end of the scale are the three banking houses with the worst records which went into foreign lending only in 1925 or later. Evidently, when the more cautious bankers refrained from expanding their loans, their place was taken by the more careless ones. As the latter did a larger share of total lending the average quality of loans declined. The rise in the average default index is in part attributable to the changed structure of the lending community.

But the big variations in the fate of loans initiated by the 11 banking houses are by no means due entirely to their different timing. The range of default indexes in the early and in the late period is as wide as for the period as a whole: from 0 to 85 percent for the first period, from 12 to 100 percent for the second (Table 12, col. 5 and 6). We have banking houses with 'good' and 'bad' results in every subperiod as well as during the period as a whole and, what is more interesting, a bank's relative position among its colleagues — as far as the quality of its foreign lending was concerned — remained much the same.[5] The five issuing houses with the best record made practically no mistakes in the first period. The default index of four rises considerably in the second period; but not one becomes as high as those of the three firms that had a high percentage of mistakes already in the early period.[6]

The parallelism of the ratios in columns 3-6 suggests that each individual banking house had a definite attitude with respect to this part of its business, an attitude that determined the quality as well as the timing of its loans. This parallelism is even more striking when we consider the aforementioned influence of random forces.

Thus from the viewpoint of the role of individual issuing houses the rise in the total default index may be regarded as the resultant of two processes. The first is a decline in the quality of loans extended by the individual banking house; this alone would account for an increase in the total default index from 17 percent in the early period to 41 percent in the late period.[7] The actual index for the late period was 60 percent, however, and the remaining part of the increase is explained by the second factor, the shift in the role of individual banks, the greater proportion of loans originated by less careful or less competent houses.

The same forces are responsible for both factors. Whatever induces a cautious banker to grant riskier loans will still more encourage a less cautious one to expand his lending and will attract new firms to such ventures. An analysis of these forces will be attempted in Chapter 6.

[5] The coefficient of rank correlation between the default indexes for the early and those for the late period is .74.

[6] Banking house 2 is the only one of the 11 whose default index does not rise in the second period. Its only defaulted loans were the Dawes and Young loans in 1924 and 1930; in 1926, 1927, and 1928, the years when most of the defaulted loans were made, it issued about half a billion dollars of foreign government bonds; not one of these was a failure.

[7] Computed by applying default indexes of the late period to the amounts of loans issued in the early period.

Chapter 5

THE RISK PREMIUM

The interpretation of the deterioration of foreign lending will rest on firmer ground if it is preceded by a statistical investigation designed to reveal clues to the motivations of investors. One question concerning motivation can be answered by empirical analysis: the investors' awareness of the increasing riskiness of their new loans. Did they not know they were embarking on ever riskier investments or did they take risk into consideration and if so to what degree?

The investor's view of the quality of his investment, his estimate of risk, is reflected in the price charged for incurring risk, the risk premium that must be offered to induce him to invest. The 'risk premium' is the difference between the yield of a specific bond and the yield of a riskless bond of the same type.[1] It will be the wider the more risky a bond seems to investors. If investors were at all aware of the declining quality of foreign bonds, risk premiums would show a rising trend over the period.

In computing risk premiums on foreign bonds, riskless rates of return are represented by David Durand's 'basic yields', yields of the absolutely best corporate bonds of all maturities, that is, minimum yields. Although basic yields "are not the equivalent of a theoretically riskless rate of return, they probably do represent the closest approximation to that rate of return attainable by empirical observation." Basic yields were devised especially for the purpose of measuring risk: "The difference between the yield of any particular bond and the basic yield was conceived as a possible measure of the bond market's appraisal of risk."[2]

Basic yields also seem preferable, for our purpose, to indexes of

---

[1] Of course there is no absolutely riskless investment; 'riskless' applies to highest grade investments where risk is so low that it may be disregarded.

[2] Basic Yields of Corporate Bonds, 1900-1942, NBER, *Technical Paper 3* (1942), pp. 1 and 21.

yields such as Moody's 'yields of 30 Aaa bonds', because the basic yields provide an array of riskless rates for bonds of different terms to maturity, whereas Moody's yield index is a single figure, constructed from bonds "of an average term of about 30 years". It is important to compare a given foreign bond with highest grade domestic bonds of the same term because maturities of foreign bonds ranged from 2 to 40 years and the corresponding difference in basic yields reached 1.55 points (in 1921). On the other hand, Durand's basic yields have the disadvantage of covering only the first quarters of calendar years; for the remaining three quarters interpolations have to be used which, of course, reduce the reliability of these data. But, all things considered, they still seem the best available indexes for the present purpose.

The average risk premiums plotted on Chart 9 are the moving averages of the weighted average differences between yields of new foreign bonds at offering prices and basic yields prevailing at the same time for bonds of like maturities. The par values of the issues serve as weights.

Among our foreign issues are several bonds on which the yield at offering is not known; therefore, a risk premium cannot be computed. These loans had to be omitted from the analysis of risk premiums, which accordingly is based upon a smaller sample than the default index. To make comparison precise we computed new default indexes for this smaller sample. They follow essentially the same course as those based on the complete sample — incidentally another indication of the stability of this measure. The two series, the risk premiums and the new default indexes, thus cover the same bond issues. One is an index of variations in the *ex ante,* the other an index of the *ex post* risk of new foreign issues.

For instance: for the first quarter of 1925 the risk premium, the measure of estimated or *ex ante* risk, was 2.18 percent; i.e., the average compensation necessary to induce American investors to assume the risks of foreign bonds issued in the first quarter of 1925 was a yield of 2.18 percent in excess of the yield obtainable on highest grade domestic bonds. The default index, the measure of actual or *ex post* risk, for the same quarter was 30 percent, showing that 30 percent of these same foreign bonds were unsound.

THE RISK PREMIUM   61

Chart 9
**Risk Premiums on Foreign Government Bonds Issued
in the United States, and Default Index
1920 — 1930**

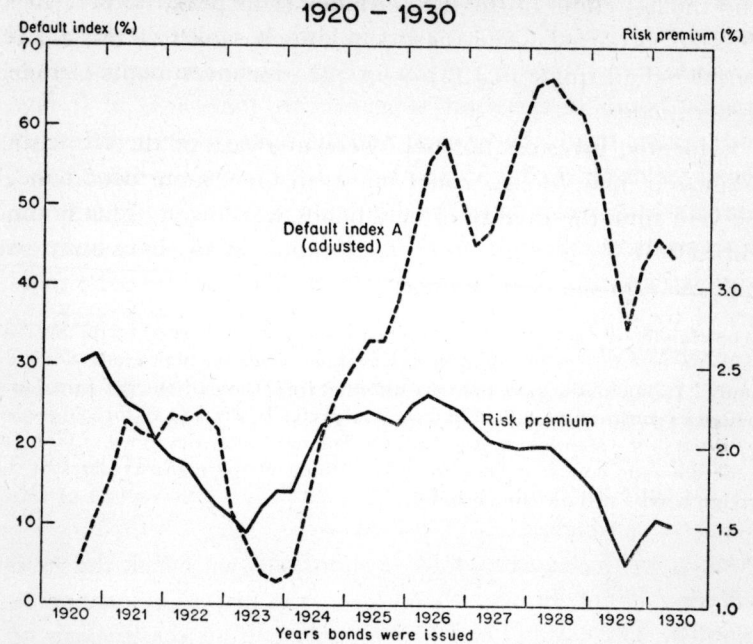

[Chart showing Default index A (adjusted) as dashed line and Risk premium as solid line, with Default index (%) on left axis from 0 to 70 and Risk premium (%) on right axis from 1.0 to 3.0, years 1920-1930 on x-axis labeled "Years bonds were issued"]

Four quarter moving averages, centered; Appendix Table 18.

Of course, this comparison is not designed to measure the extent to which losses were covered by risk premiums.[3] We are not concerned with this question because answering it throws no light on changes in loan quality. There is no doubt that risk premiums of early loans covered a larger part of losses than those of later ones, since loss depends so largely on the time interval between flotation and default. Nothing could be gained by proving this obvious fact. What matters here is only the change in the relation of the risk premium to the default index, since this is an indicator of the change in investors' attitudes.

The contrast between the rapid rise in the riskiness of loans and the relative stability and, in 1927-28, even downward tendency, of risk premiums is striking (Chart 9). Between 1925 and 1926

[3] For a detailed analysis of the financial outcome of the loans, based on the situation at the close of 1935, see Madden et al., op. cit., Ch. VIII.

the default index rose from 30 to 58 percent, while the risk premium advanced only a trifle — from 2.18 to 2.32 percent. And the last climb of the default index to its peak, 66 percent in 1927-28, occurred while the risk premium sank to 2.00, a level considered adequate in 1921 or in 1924 for investments of much higher quality.

Evidently, investors not only were unaware of the increasing riskiness of new foreign issues but even grew more confident at the very time the quality of new bonds was lowest. This finding will help us to interpret the deterioration of foreign credit; we shall use it in the next chapter.[4]

[4] The *Handbook* (op. cit., p. 44) offers an index of the "excess of the average yields on new foreign bonds over the average yields on high-grade domestic bonds." Its fluctuations are not very different from those of our risk premiums, though its construction differs in several respects: It refers to all foreign securities listed in the *Handbook;* it utilizes the Standard Statistics index of 60 high-grade domestic bonds; it does not take account of the maturity dates of the foreign bonds; it is an annual index.

Chapter 6

AN INTERPRETATION

We shall now attempt to interpret the statistical results, to uncover their meaning by supplementing the statistics with an analytical description of foreign lending. The forces at work in the process of credit deterioration are often dealt with under the elusive title of 'optimism'. However, this is no more than a label and tells little about what really goes on. We shall try to dig a bit deeper and to reveal the interplay of factors hidden behind 'optimism'.

Though our analysis is confined to foreign loans and to a short period its relevance need not end there. Its results may well reveal some features of credit expansion in general. If so, it may contribute to the understanding of business cycles.[1]

1 *The Picture of Change*

THE EARLY DAYS

The early part of the period under review begins with the end of World War I. No exact date can be set for the end of this period or the beginning of the 'late period'. It depends upon the particular borrower and lender in question. Roughly 1920-24 may be called the early period, 1925 brought the transition, and 1926-29 may be called the late period.

Even the very first step in the process of foreign lending, trivial as it may seem, is symptomatic, because the procedure was later entirely reversed, as we shall see. ". . . it was customary . . . in the

---

[1] The following is based in part on hearings held by the Senate Committee on Finance, 72d Cong., 1st Sess., on the 'Sale of Foreign Bonds or Securities in the United States' from December 18, 1931 to February 10, 1932. Officials and partners of leading investment banking houses, government officials and financial experts testified at these hearings and submitted data on foreign loans. Various reforms were later made in part by individual bankers on their own initiative and in part by government regulation. In particular the investment banking business was restricted to firms not affiliated with commercial banks.

early days . . . for the Government to entrust to some individual in the country concerned the task of coming to New York and negotiating the loan for the province, state, or municipality . . . the individual concerned was told by the finance minister . . . to see what he could do toward getting a loan. . . ."[2]

In New York it was not easy for the agents of foreign countries to obtain a loan. Many were unsuccessful. Many bankers "declined to have anything to do with this matter. And it was a very difficult business".[3] If a banker was disposed to grant a loan he would weigh the risk carefully and come to a decision slowly.

Once a banker undertook to float a foreign loan he had to convince the public of its safety. "And it took . . . a process of enlightenment and explanation, for instance, to point out why the obligation of the French Government . . . was absolutely good. . . ."[4] The public did not know much about foreign countries or cities. For example, ". . . at that time the City of Christiania [Oslo] was very little known here, and a great deal of work had to be done in explaining it, in sending out literature, and so forth."[5] "And it was a most difficult business because a good many people in our country did not know where Hungary was. We published books with pictures . . . we had a regular campaign in order to let the public know the circumstances. We got some men to make speeches and to explain to the people what the purpose of the loan was. It was quite a campaign."[6]

The necessity for propaganda made the loans more expensive to float and increased the spread, the difference between the price paid the issuer and the price paid by investors, the issuing banker had to charge. The spread was widened further by the riskiness of the business for the banker, owing to the uncertain saleability of the bonds. Again and again at the hearings held by the Senate Finance Committee in 1932 the bankers were asked why the

[2] From the testimony of Henry C. Breck, partner, J. and W. Seligman & Co., Hearings, p. 1307.
[3] James Speyer of Speyer & Co., ibid., p. 618.
[4] Thomas W. Lamont of J. P. Morgan & Co., ibid., p. 20.
[5] Otto H. Kahn, member of the banking house of Kuhn, Loeb & Co., ibid., p. 126.
[6] Mr. Speyer, ibid., p. 616.

AN INTERPRETATION

spread had to be so high at first and could be so much reduced later. The answer was always: ". . . we had to have a larger spread in the early postwar years. . . ." because we risked being unable to sell the bonds and because our selling costs were high. Yields too, of course, had to be high in order to win over the reluctant investing public.

Thus in the early days a borrower had to seek out a banker who would be willing to lend. The banker in turn had to convince the investing public of the high quality of the bonds he wanted to sell. And the resistance of both banker and public had to be overcome by high yields and large spreads.

THE LATE PERIOD

In the late period this process was reversed from the very first step. The borrower no longer sends his man to New York; now the New York banker sends his representatives to foreign capitals. The testimony at the Senate hearings in 1931-32 is enlightening. Senator Johnson: ". . . you reversed the processes of the ordinary mode of conducting a banking business; you had in these last few years the lenders going to the borrowers. . . ?" Frederick Strauss, partner, J. & W. Seligman & Co.: "Yes, sir." Senator: "And in that fashion they accelerated, stimulated, increased loans of various political subdivisions, Governments, industrial enterprises, and the like; is not that correct?" Mr. Strauss: "That was the effect of it; yes."[7] James C. Corliss, then specialist, Latin American Finance, Department of Commerce, also describes how a great many representatives of American financial houses tried to get loans in a number of countries. The bankers' agents not only tried to negotiate given loans but used high pressure salesmanship to find borrowers. Mr. Corliss: "There was very keen competition in a great many countries for those loans." Senator: "Will you explain what you mean by keen competition. . . ?" Mr. Corliss: "At one time in Colombia there were something like 29 representatives, I was told."[8] The competition was brought out by other witnesses as well. Senator: "Were there others who were competing with you for the loan there?" F. J. Lisman: "We understood there were

[7] Ibid., p. 1324.   [8] Ibid., p. 845-6.

several banking houses there." Senator: "All of them trying to get the loan from the Peruvian Government?" Mr. Lisman: "As usual." Senator: "That is so all over Latin America?" Mr. Lisman: "It was so during the period from 1925-28, all over, I would say."[9] The scope of this development was indicated in another exchange. Senator: "There were many firms . . . who had their agents and their representatives in different places in Latin America seeking to obtain governmental loans . . . is not that true?" Mr. Strauss: "Yes; but it is also true that those things existed not only in Latin America, but the world over. . . ."[10]

This last remark is confirmed by Mr. Lamont in a speech in 1927: "I have in mind the reports that I have recently heard of American bankers and firms competing on almost a violent scale for the purpose of obtaining loans in various foreign money markets overseas. Naturally it is a tempting thing for certain of the European Governments to find a horde of American bankers sitting on their doorsteps offering them money. . . . That sort of competition tends to insecurity and unsound practice."[11]

Oliver C. Townsend, Commercial Attache at Lima, Peru, from 1926 to 1929 reveals something of the climate of loan negotiations of this period and of the "general promotion atmosphere" in a memorandum dated February 10, 1927 to the United States Ambassador to Peru: "Tuesday night's dinner, given at the Hotel Bolivar by S. A. MacGinnis to fifty-odd guests, was a fair sample of what the local society folk are treated to at rather close intervals, namely, entertainment by promoters. . . . Our host . . . is here with a big entertainment fund in the interest of . . . a New York banking firm, to bid on the securities shortly to be issued. . . ."[12]

The keen competition for loans led to bribery and commissions for all who helped or claimed they helped to obtain them. Yet the bankers' spread dropped considerably because selling costs declined

---

[9] Frederick J. Lisman, F. J. Lisman & Co., ibid., p. 1775.
[10] Ibid., pp. 1323-4. For a lively description of competition among bankers for foreign loans and other aspects of unwise lending, see Max Winkler, op. cit., Ch. IV and V.
[11] Quoted in the Hearings, p. 25.   [12] Ibid., p. 1611.

AN INTERPRETATION

sharply and there was little risk of getting stuck with the bonds. Selling bonds was no longer a problem. For instance, the spread declined from 6½ to 5½ points between March and December 1927 for Peruvian bonds; from 13 to 8 points between 1925 and 1927 for two loans to Cauca Valley, Colombia. "At that period, say, from 1924 to and including 1928, the bond market was extremely eager and very receptive, for bonds especially those yielding high rates of interest. . . ."[13]

Every aspect of foreign lending had changed. Senator: "The last few years of your business are not comparable with the kind of business or the mode in which you conducted your business in prior years?" Mr. Strauss: "That is quite true, Senator." ". . . the point you are making is about the business methods, the change that has come about. It would not have been natural 10 or 20 years ago."[14]

Thus, in the late period the lender sought out the borrower, offering every conceivable concession to attract him. The public in turn was no less eager to take the bonds from the bankers than the bankers were to find borrowers.

Comparing the two periods we find the characteristics typical of a change from a buyers' to a sellers' market, where the buyers correspond to the lenders and the sellers to the borrowers: depressed prices, high quality of goods, high selling costs in the former; high prices, low quality of goods, low selling costs in the latter. The deteriorating quality of loans fits perfectly into the general picture.

The situation would have been much worse had not part of the banking community resisted the temptation of easy profits and preferred fewer rather than low quality bonds, as was shown in the analysis of individual banking firms in Chapter 4. In this connection the testimony of Grosvenor M. Jones, then Chief, Finance and Investment Division, Department of Commerce, is of interest. Senator: "During the last few years . . . investment houses and the like have indulged in the keenest competition to obtain from the South American Governments and from Latin America the securities for flotation in this country, have they not?"

[13] Mr. Kahn, ibid., p. 394. [14] Ibid., pp. 1323 and 1325.

Mr. Jones: "In general, I think there are two notable exceptions." Senator: "Two notable exceptions. I think, in justice to those two, we ought to state them." Mr. Jones: "I will not say that they are the only exceptions; but J. P. Morgan and Co., and Kuhn, Loeb and Co. have followed, more or less, the English tradition of the borrower seeking the lender rather than the lender seeking the borrower."[15] This agrees with the statistical findings. The two banking houses Mr. Jones names are the only ones that reduced their lending in the second half of the period; moreover, their default indexes are the second and the third lowest of the group investigated (Ch. 4).

2 Analysis of Change

Though the world situation at the time might lead one to suppose it, pressure on the part of borrowers was not a reason for the deterioration of loans.[16] In the 2,000 odd pages of the Senate Hearings foreign political pressure, propaganda, or bribery to induce American bankers to grant an increasing volume of loans is not mentioned once, but there are numerous accusations against American bankers of having used such means to force loans on foreign countries.

Is the explanation of the deterioration of the quality of credit simply that early borrowers had an opportunity during the favorable twenties to get their finances into shape to withstand serious depression, while late borrowers were caught in the depression before they had a chance to put their house in order? Such an argument implies that a major part of 'bad' loans was used to fortify initially weak economies of debtor countries. But such was not the case. The Latin American economies emerged from World War I greatly strengthened; their loans were not needed for restoration or recovery, nor used to build up resistance against depression. German and eastern European debtors were in a different

---

[15] Ibid., pp. 742-3.
[16] See our interpretation of foreign loan cycles (Ch. 1) which also suggests that forces arising here rather than abroad were decisive in foreign lending.

The picture confirms also what we would expect in theory. An increasing volume of loans accompanied by rising prices to lenders means that the demand curve, representing in this case the lenders, must have shifted to the right.

situation. But in view of their economic policies in general and the improvident use they frequently made of their loans, it is hard to believe that the lapse of a few more years would have put them in a position where they could have avoided default. Indeed, one might well argue that the longer some debtors were able to borrow the less were they prepared for a reversal of economic conditions.

The invalidity of the argument that late borrowers were at a disadvantage when the depression came and that this was itself the cause of the high rate of defaults is demonstrated by the recent history of foreign bonds. As we noted above, despite war prosperity and greatly increased dollar exports all South American countries in default in 1937 were still in default in 1949. Certainly, their present default cannot be explained by their having borrowed too late in the twenties. Nor can the maintenance of full service by Belgium, France, Norway despite enormous war damage be ascribed to their having borrowed early in the twenties.

The high proportion of defaulted loans among issues of the late twenties is not a necessary consequence of their date of issue. To understand the deterioration we must know why the proportion of loans that went to borrowers prone to default rose.

It would be in line with the theory of an increasing shortage of investment opportunities to suggest that 'there are just so many good loans' and, therefore, a surplus of investible funds can only be employed in making unsound ones. At first blush this reasoning seems quite plausible. It might be elaborated along these lines: After World War I nations that had formerly exported capital needed loans for a short while. These were the sound loans of the first period. Later these nations became able once more to take care of their own needs and even to regain their former position as capital exporters, driving the United States as the youngest among the lending nations into the least desirable markets.

Convincing as this may sound, the evidence is against it. When investors are confronted with a lack of sound investment opportunities for their accumulating funds, the pressure on the market for high-grade bonds drives their prices up. To the individual investor, 'scarcity of sound loans' can mean only that their prices are so high as to make investment in riskier but cheaper bonds seem preferable. If, on the contrary, prices of riskier investments rose more than those of low risk investments, we can hardly say that lack of the latter forced investors into the former.

What are the facts in our case? Basic yields on 30-year bonds, which may be regarded as representative for the high-grade domestic bond market, declined from 4.50 to 4.05 percent between 1925 and 1928. In other words, the 'lack of sound loans' meant that the investor had to accept a 10 percent decline in yield. Let us compare developments in the market for foreign bonds. In 1925 the average risk premium for foreign issues, 30 percent of which subsequently proved unsound, was 2.18 percent. In 1928 a crop of foreign bonds, 65 percent of which were failures, could be sold to yield not more than a 2.00 percent risk premium. Thus investors accepted an 8 percent reduction in risk premium for a much riskier investment at the very time they accepted only a 10 percent reduction of yields on high-grade investments of constant quality. Prices of risky foreign bonds, in other words, rose relatively more than prices of high-grade domestic bonds. Hence it cannot be said that investors were 'forced' to resort to risky investments.

High-grade foreign loans might have been expanded if American investors had accepted a more drastic cut in their yields. For instance, the shrinkage in the volume of Canadian loans when total foreign lending reached its peak can probably be attributed to unfavorable conditions for low risk investment in the United States. The public's demand for high yielding bonds excluded borrowers who offered lower yields. To a certain extent the lower grade bonds drove the high-grade bonds from the market.

Lack of good loans cannot account for the mounting proportion of mistakes. Another element is necessary to understand what happened: the delusions of the investors concerning the safety of their loans. Investors bought low-grade bonds because they were not aware of the risks they were incurring and it was their mistaken judgment that kept the prices of high-grade bonds relatively low. These delusions cannot be attributed to the influence of a few fraudulent investment bankers, as has sometimes been suggested. Their roots were deeper and can be understood only by considering the entire economic climate of the 1920's.

The most important single factor leading investors to be less cautious was the complete absence of defaults on foreign government bonds during this entire period. In the early years few unsound loans had been issued and even these few were not defaulted during the mild contractions of the 1920's. (In this respect the severe depression of 1920-21 was no different from the later mild ones; at this time, of course, American bankers had only just begun to lend abroad.) The partial character of liquidation of unsuccessful investments during several successive mild contractions has often been regarded as one of the causes of the ensuing severe depression. In foreign loans there was not even a partial 'liquidation'. Whatever errors were made did not become apparent and bad risks accumulated through the decade. The confidence of bankers and public grew as time passed and no losses were incurred.

Another factor that bred illusions was the considerable profit made by a great number of investors during a long period. Moreover, these gains furnished funds for more investment of the same kind. The longer this period of continuous gains and no losses lasted, the more were people inclined to believe there was no end in sight. The growing distance from the last severe depression dimmed their memory of past catastrophies. Even those who were cycle-conscious were reassured by the mild contractions of the 1920's, which passed without inflicting losses on foreign bondholders and left the impression that severe depressions were a thing of the past, something that had been overcome. The very absence of a severe depression over such a long period might have caused apprehension. But it had the opposite effect: the longer a telling depression was avoided the greater the confidence in the future became. This is not to say that every banker or investor shared these views but overconfidence set the tone.

These delusions had of course a cumulative effect. The new lending they encouraged was used to pay old debts when other funds were not available, thereby prolonging the life of bad debtors, postponing defaults, and in turn adding to the delusions.

What was the American government's role in all this? Was it more foresighted than bankers and investors? According to James

W. Angell, the government "has influenced the course of international finance in an extraordinarily wide variety of ways."[17] Did this influence contribute to or mitigate the decline in loan quality? Concerning the impact of government policies on Latin American, Canadian and Far Eastern loans, Angell comes to the following conclusion: "Undoubtedly, the great majority of the present American commitments in these regions, made chiefly since the war, *would have been effected even had the government remained entirely passive*. The war left the United States, for a number of years, as the only large source of exportable capital to which the rest of the world could turn. No action by the United States Government was needed to induce American business men to reach for the commercial and financial opportunities created by this situation."[18]

It seems probable that capital exports would on the whole have been smaller without the government's encouragement, though in a few cases the government placed an embargo on capital exports. But whether more sound or unsound loans were promoted we do not know.

3 *Role of the Banking Houses*

As the decision of the issuing banker is directly responsible for each loan we can begin to describe his role by analyzing this decision and its motivation. The business of the banker is to lend. The driving force in his decisions is the prospect of profits. But to protect the goodwill of his firm he must refrain from business that might entail losses for his customers. Every loan decision is the outcome of a process of weighing these conflicting motives against each other. Banks are the apparatus designed to do this weighing. In our case this apparatus worked well for a while; the restraining force of risk was strong enough to prevent mistakes except for a small percentage of loans. This same apparatus functioned much less well in the late twenties as the restraining force of risk declined.

[17] *Financial Foreign Policy of the United States* (A Report to the Second International Studies Conference on the State and Economic Life, London, 1933. Prepared for the American Committee appointed by the Council on Foreign Relations, 1933), p. 123.
[18] Ibid., p. 98, italics mine.

AN INTERPRETATION

Confining our discussion to two factors in the bankers' decisions, risk and profit, is not to deny the influence of others. Undoubtedly a few loans were floated in deference to the wishes of the American government; others were granted because the bankers hoped to win the favor of the government of a country where they had other large investments; personal relations with foreign bankers may occasionally have had some influence; and so forth. But considerations of this kind operated only in isolated cases and were neither general nor powerful enough to explain the drastic deterioration in loan quality during the 1920's.

a) BANKING ESTIMATES OF RISK[19]

Without attempting a complete enumeration, we wish to give a general idea of the large number of factors bankers considered in estimating the soundness of a loan. The charge that most private bankers lacked information about their debtors and that the quality of credit could have been markedly improved if loans had been investigated more carefully does not seem to be supported by the facts. We do not find evidence that bankers were generally ignorant of the factors considered relevant for the soundness of loans. These are some of the factors the bankers took into consideration: 1) The political situation: prospects of peace or war, stability of the foreign government, relations between the United States and the debtor country, etc. 2) Character of the borrowing nation: its willingness to make sacrifices in order to pay its debts. This is important because some nations take advantage of any pretext to avoid paying which, since it is not feasible to force payment of foreign debts, is as bad as incapacity to pay. Other nations, on the contrary, go to great lengths to pay their debts. 3) The general economic situation of the debtor country: This would involve a careful analysis of: "Its past debt record. ... Its record of income and expenditures for a period of from 5 to 10 years preceding the time at which the loan is being considered, and its budget for the succeeding year or two years. Its import and export statistics for the past 5 or 10 years and an analysis of its 'invisible' trade, if any. Its national debt both on a total and a per capita basis.

[19] 'Risk' always means risk of default, not the risk the banker runs of not being able to sell the issue.

Its national wealth. Its fiscal position as to its holdings of gold or the gold holdings of its central bank in relation to its outstanding currency. . . . Value of its actual or potential trade with the United States. . . ."[20]

This point, the economic position of the nation, was usually deemed to be the most important factor even when the loan was granted to a private borrower.[21]

4) The particular economic position of the borrowing corporation:[22] "First we make a detailed study . . . of the following: Nature and scope of the company's activity. Territory served. Property and business . . . Competition . . . Public relations. Governmental and State regulation. Possibilities of future growth. Second, a study of ownership and management of the company. Third, a detailed study of an examination and appraisal of properties by independent American engineers. Fourth, a detailed study of examination and audit of earnings and balance sheet position of the company, covering a period of years, by American certified public accountants. Fifth, a detailed study of various legal aspects of the situation investigated by our counsel. . . ."[23]

On the points mentioned under 1-4 bankers collected information in various ways. The Department of Commerce bulletins which were based on reports by foreign service officers of the government were widely used. Many bankers sent experts into the borrowing countries, consulted with bankers of these countries, and checked their conclusions against the opinions of such experts as S. Parker Gilbert, Agent General for Reparation Payments, and Hjalmar Schacht,[24] or against the attitude of England and Holland, as the older lender nations.

5) Terms of the loan: many bankers thought the safety of a loan could be increased by inserting certain provisions in the contract. For example, the League of Nations loans contained far-reaching

[20] Memorandum from Kuhn, Loeb & Co., Hearings, p. 293.
[21] See, for instance, Mr. Lamont, ibid., p. 48.
[22] This factor is not without bearing on our analysis because the bonds investigated include government guaranteed corporate issues.
[23] E. C. Granberry, Vice Chairman, Board of Directors, Chase, Harris, Forbes Corporation; ibid., p. 526.
[24] Ibid., p. 102.

AN INTERPRETATION 75

provisions to ensure their safety: guarantees by several other nations; priority over all other obligations; the obligation of the debtor nation to balance its budget and provisions for financial control to enforce this.

Sometimes the borrowing country pledged a certain source of revenue as security for the service of the loan or the loan was paid in instalments each of which was contingent upon the maintenance of a balanced budget,[25] or the country simply promised to balance its budget.

In order to increase the safety of a loan the bankers sometimes stipulated that it should be used for some specific productive purpose yielding a revenue that would ensure its service. Some contracts went so far as to provide for control over the expenditure of the money; e.g., in Cuba the money was not paid to the government at all but directly to the contractors against certificates of work done; i.e., it was not available for other purposes.[26]

This recital may suffice to illustrate the variety of factors the bankers said they examined and on which they based their judgments of the safety of their loans. Their contention is well supported. Most convincing are the statements by witnesses at the Senate Hearings who otherwise sharply criticized the bankers. They do not charge that loans were issued in ignorance of the relevant facts; on the contrary, they charge that the bankers were aware of unfavorable circumstances yet issued loans anyway. The declaration of the Committee on Banking and Currency that the bankers "failed to examine, or examined only perfunctorily, economic conditions in foreign countries" seems hardly justified.[27] Ignorance was not in general the cause of the mistakes in foreign lending.

But if all the circumstances of the loan, the debtor, his country, and the world in general were taken into account, why did the

[25] See, for instance, ibid., pp. 1649 ff.
[26] "We did feel an added security in the fact that the moneys we provided would be paid over to the construction contractors themselves...." A. M. Williams, of Rushmore, Bisbee & Stern, Attorneys for the Chase National Bank, ibid., p. 1964.
[27] Stock Exchange Practices, Report of the Committee on Banking and Currency, 73rd Cong., 1934, Senate Report No. 1455, p. 126.

correctness of the bankers' judgment vary so much over time? Why was it sound on the whole at one time and wide of the mark at another? Evidently differences in interpretation of the facts are responsible. The most detailed study of the position of a debtor informs us only about his past and present. It is when we project into the future that we are likely to make mistakes. And if more mistakes are made at one time than at another, projecting into the future must be easier and thus more reliable at some times than at others.

In the first part of our period when the world was gradually recovering from World War I it was conservative to expect this to continue for some time. But in the later period of rapid expansion it was reckless to project the favorable trends into the future. This, however, was precisely what many bankers did.

An example will illustrate how careful information led to wrong conclusions because the banker expected current trends to continue into the future and disregarded inflationary conditions. To show the soundness of Peru's economy a banker reasoned: "After these bonds were issued . . . the total annual service charges on the external funded debt amounted to approximately 20 percent of the average ordinary revenues for the preceding three years (1925, 1926 and 1927). . . . The Peruvian Government's ordinary revenues for 1928 were 20 percent greater than for 1926, and the excess of its expenditures . . . over such revenues was substantially less than for 1926. Exports were 31 percent greater, the excess of exports over imports 215 percent greater, the production of cotton 2 percent greater, sugar 4 percent less, copper 21 percent greater and petroleum exports 6 percent greater than in 1926. . . . As important as, if not more important than, the then favorable current position of Peru were the trends during a period of years. These trends were favorable, too, as indicated by the fact that between 1913 and 1926 ordinary revenues of the Government had increased 186 percent, exports 162 percent, the excess of exports over imports 45 percent. . . ."[28]

The bankers apparently took little account of the probability that these 'favorable trends' were unlikely to continue when, as

[28] Statement of J. & W. Seligman & Co.; Hearings, pp. 2118-9.

AN INTERPRETATION 77

in this case, they were based on an enormous expansion of bank credit. Some bankers even evolved a formula that implied the assumption of continued inflation. "They said that if loan charges were covered three times by revenues then the loan was sound."[29] But revenues of a country that borrows heavily do not indicate its future ability to pay.

There were exceptions, of course. Some bankers judged the situation correctly and refrained from lending to countries where inflationary conditions prevailed.[30] A few even went so far as to warn their colleagues. For instance, in 1927 Mr. Lamont warned against "indiscriminate lending and indiscriminate borrowing".[31]

Experts too raised their voices. In his memorandum of 1927 on reparations, for instance, S. Parker Gilbert brought together "the accumulating evidences of overspending and overborrowing on the part of the German public authorities, and some of the indications of artificial stimulation and overexpansion that are already manifesting themselves". He concluded: "These tendencies, if allowed to continue unchecked, are almost certain . . . to lead to severe economic reaction and depression. . . ."[32]

Occasionally a warning came from the borrowing countries themselves: ". . . the president of the Reserve Bank of Peru . . . came up to New York, and told the bankers that they were lending far too much, and that they should at least cut their loans in half. That was in 1927, before they made their first loan."[33]

Yet most of these warnings were in more or less general terms and were often dismissed as not applying to the particular loans bankers were about to make. Their attitude may seem somewhat surprising since, logically, we would expect their caution to grow, instead of decrease, with the distance from the last severe depression. Their awareness that loans are tested in times of severe depression and that the absence of defaults at other times does not prove

---

[29] Lawrence Dennis, connected with J. & W. Seligman & Co., 1928-30, ibid., p. 1591.
[30] This is one important source of differences between default indexes of individual banks; see Ch. 4.
[31] Hearings, p. 25.
[32] Ibid., p. 897; cf. also Max Winkler, op. cit.
[33] Lawrence Dennis, Hearings, p. 1601.

that all loans are sound should have functioned as a brake on the over-optimism of the public. This it did, to some degree. But to a large extent the bankers were influenced by current favorable aspects of economic developments. The spell of the long defaultless period made them forget that "During the nineteenth century every major downward swing of the business cycle caused the failure of governments and other foreign borrowers to meet their external obligations".[34] Or, if the disasters of the past were remembered they were discounted in the belief that modern economic policy was able to prevent severe depressions, a belief strengthened by the mildness of recent contractions. A reversal of favorable trends was feared less rather than more as time wore on and current trends were confidently projected into the future. As world conditions improved, expectations grew more and more optimistic, i.e., more and more incorrect. Thus the bankers' estimates of risk were an important factor in the decline of loan quality.

b) THE IMPORTANCE OF RISK

Another possible source of variation in the quality of loans is the different weight bankers place upon risk at different times. To determine the role of risk in the decisions of bankers let us listen first to what they themselves say. They are virtually unanimous that no banker ever issued a loan he did not consider safe: Mr. Strauss: ". . . we have never brought out a bond issue that we did not believe at the time was a safe investment; . . . no loans were undertaken, in spite of the madness that you speak of, that were not believed to be safe." Mr. Lamont: ". . . we never issue a bond unless we believe it to be good." Mr. Kahn: ". . . I can say for my house that for every issue that we made we declined six others, or probably more, because we always want to be sure that what we offer is intrinsically sound. . . ." Mr. Lamont: ". . . it was a very attractive investment. That is, if you had faith in the future of the country. And if you did not, it would not be attractive on any basis."[35]

The bankers stress also their lasting interest in their bonds. Senator: ". . . and have you any further interest in those bonds?" Mr.

[34] Madden et al., op. cit., p. 107.
[35] Hearings, pp. 1322, 1324, 40, 342, 49-50.

Kahn: "We have an interest in those bonds until they are repaid according to their due date. We consider that we are under a permanent moral liability to do what we can for the protection of those bonds."[36] Mr. Granberry: ". . . in case a bond is in default quite naturally the original issuing house, or houses as the case may be, use their best efforts, and both time and money, to try to correct the default and make the bond good." Senator: "You do not mean to say that you put your capital into defaulted interest or principal of bonds." Mr. Granberry: "We put our money more or less into defaulted situations to try to make them good."[37] Mr. Speyer: "And that responsibility continues on for 20 or 30 years. . . . The sums of money that we spend in looking after these things, and trying to straighten them out, nobody knows anything about."[38] And again Mr. Kahn: "The issuing house considers it its responsibility to do everything in its power to reconstitute and reestablish the solvency and the good credit of the property, to protect the bondholders . . . to give its efforts, its experience, its ability fairly and properly to deal with the situation which a default has created."[39]

A banker has good reason to examine carefully what he sells and to try to protect his customers from losses. "The banker's prosperity, indeed his very existence, depends on the confidence of the public. If he has not got that . . . his business will shrink to negligible proportions, if not fail completely. Confidence . . . must be acquired every day by the way you conduct your business. . . ."[40] Of few goods is the buyer less able to gauge the true value than of foreign bonds. He must rely largely upon the banker's reputation, on his 'ethical trade mark' which, therefore, will be more important to the banker's business than, e.g., that of a shoe dealer's to his.

Even more convincing than the banker's testimony or our reasoning about the role of safety are the facts mentioned in the preceding section, i.e., the great trouble and expense to which bankers go to assure themselves that their loans are sound.

Of course, the importance attached to risk varies greatly from

[36] Ibid., p. 135.
[37] Ibid., p. 519.
[38] Ibid., p. 617.
[39] Ibid., p. 128.
[40] Mr. Kahn, ibid., p. 352.

one banking firm to another.[41] The better the name of a firm, the more reason it has to protect it. A new firm may be more likely to try to 'make hay while the sun shines'. And in addition to the banker's self-interest his feeling of social responsibility will, to a larger or smaller degree, impel him to look to the safety of his loans.

Does the power of risk as a brake vary over time? That may depend upon the strength of the factor discussed in the next section: public demand for foreign issues.

4 *The Demand of the Public*

a) WHO IS 'THE PUBLIC'?

We know little about investors in foreign bonds. In the opinion of Dwight W. Morrow "The person who invests in foreign bonds is probably the same person who invests in domestic bonds".[42] But this does not tell us much and may not be altogether correct.[43] The attitudes of individual investors differ widely and vary continuously. Some would not touch foreign bonds under any circumstances ('isolationist investors'), others buy only the issues of countries that have proved to be reliable debtors, a third type demands exceedingly high yields, and so forth. Demand for any given loan at any given time will be the resultant of all these tendencies.

There seem to have been no empirical investigations into the type and number of foreign bond buyers except some on a very small scale undertaken by Senator Morrow in 1927. His analysis of the sales of 24 investment houses covering 5 foreign government loans showed that more than 85 percent of the purchases were in small amounts ranging from $100 to $5,000, and that approximately half of these 5 issues went to these small investors.[44]

Another bit of information can be gleaned from registrations of bondholders with protective committees. The Foreign Bondholders Protective Council reports: "The Committee of Bondholders for the Republic of Chile Bonds has included in the registrations

[41] Differences in the regard for risk seem to be one of the chief reasons for the wide differences between the default indexes of different banking houses (see Ch. 4).
[42] Who Buys Foreign Bonds? *Foreign Affairs,* January 1927.
[43] See Ch. 1, Sec. 5.
[44] Hearings, pp. 152-4.

with that Committee individual bondholders, banks, trust funds, schools, colleges, universities, theological seminaries, churches, church societies, libraries, hospitals, memorial homes, foundations, orphanages, Y.M.C.A.'s, and cemetery associations. Every state in the United States, one territory of the United States, the District of Columbia, and thirty foreign countries are represented in the registrations so far received. While a number of the registrants hold substantial amounts of bonds, the average holding is very small, showing an extremely wide distribution of these bonds . . . the average holding of . . . 96% of registrants is $800 worth of bonds per person."[45]

Foreign security holders were estimated to exceed 1.5 million in 1932.[46] The SEC has estimated that between 600,000 and 700,000 investors held defaulted foreign bonds in 1937. In any case there seems to be general agreement that many small investors held foreign bonds. Unlike the large investor, the small investor cannot insure against losses by diversifying his investments. Moreover, he will often be unable to wait and thus ultimately to recover all or part of his loss. As he has to take his full loss, his mistake or carelessness in purchasing a risky bond is relatively greater than would be that of a big investor.

b) WHY DOES THE PUBLIC BUY FOREIGN BONDS?

Why did large numbers of investors deem foreign bonds safe investments? Why were they so confident that a foreign country or town, whose name they had hardly known a few months earlier, would be willing and able to keep up the service of its loans for 20 or 30 years?

It has been said that "faith in the banker was the only measuring rod for the investor"; that "Those bonds were bought by Tom, Dick and Harry . . . without any reference to the solidity or the solvency of the bonds . . . , but entirely on the faith of the house issuing them in New York."[47]

Doubtless the bankers' confidence reinforced that of the public and their propaganda influenced investors. But this is only part of the story. Let us remember that this "faith in the banker" did

[45] Foreign Bondholders Protective Council, *Annual Report, 1935,* p. 99.
[46] Charles E. Mitchell, Chairman, National City Bank, Hearings, p. 70.
[47] Ibid., pp. 325, 352.

not always exist, that the public did not always buy everything the bankers offered. In our description of the early period we stressed the great efforts bankers made and the expenses they incurred in creating a market for foreign bonds. Evidently at that time they could not rely on the public's faith and expect it to buy whatever they offered. They had to refuse many transactions because they feared they would not be able to convince the public of their safety and as a rule could float only sound issues with relatively high yields.

Reliance on the banker was, then, itself the product of a certain period. Why did the public trust its bankers precisely between 1925 and 1928? Why should thousands of individuals develop such a curious unquestioning faith in bankers? The answer is that the public's attitude was not due to any mysterious faith but was caused by the very factors that determined the bankers' attitude. And these factors swayed the public without being checked by competence and responsibility. Investors in foreign bonds had not suffered any losses for a long time; on the contrary, they had repeatedly made sizable profits. This pleasant state came to be regarded as normal; investors assumed the world had entered a period of permanent defaultless prosperity.

Many events served to substantiate this belief. The League of Nations and the Locarno Pacts seemed to open peaceful prospects. Europe had recovered economically, runaway inflation had been stopped in every country, currencies were stable. Confidence in the world in general was the basis for the confidence of both banker and investor.[48]

c) HOW DID THE CHANGE IN THE PUBLIC'S ATTITUDE AFFECT THE BANKERS?

Bankers base their expectations of demand on their own and their colleagues' day to day experience. To foresee potential demand is difficult when a country is taking its first steps in the international

---

[48] This is shown also by the public's attitude toward other types of relatively risky investment where reliance on the banker played a less important role, e.g., domestic common stock issues. Plentiful credit and mistaken ideas about the future raised the demand for riskier investments and as a result quality quite probably deteriorated in many fields.

capital market or after a period of inactivity in the market. It is easier and forecasts are more reliable when the bankers know how the market reacted to similar loans a short time before. They observe and base their judgment on significant symptoms, such as the attitude of the bond market in general and in regard to the bonds of the specific country, the possibility of catching a favorable moment, etc.

Prospect of sufficient demand is a prerequisite for floating a loan. Therefore, the changed outlook of the public, itself greatly influenced by the bankers, had grave repercussions on the bankers' position. We have seen above how in the early twenties the uncertainty of demand, investors' reluctance to buy, were constantly on bankers' minds, and how this tended to discourage flotations or caused extra outlay and trouble when an issue was finally decided upon.

In the late period the bankers stress the influence of the public's attitude on them more than anything else in their testimony.[49] The public's eagerness is mentioned again and again as the motive for floating bonds. Senator: "Seeking in every way to obtain such loans as you could for flotation here?" Mr. Lisman: "To satisfy the public demand for securities."[50] Senator: "What was it that led to the extraordinarily keen competition among international bankers for South American loans?" Mr. Breck: "I think it was an appetite on the part of the American public to buy foreign loans."[51]

Country banks, tempted by high yields, acted like the general public and considered the bonds "to be sound and safe investments. . . ." "They were anxious to take them. They asked for them. These little bankers wanted to be in bond syndicates just as the big bankers wanted to be, because 90 percent and more of such syndicates at that time turned out to be profitable." They

[49] The fluctuations in the volume of foreign loan flotations (see Ch. 1) indicate that the public's attitude varied also within each period; that it was always easier to sell foreign bonds in times of domestic recession than in times of expansion when domestic stocks absorbed more of the available funds. However, these shorter demand fluctuations within the early and within the late period appear to have impressed the bankers far less than the big increase in demand between the two periods.

[50] Hearings, p. 1775.   [51] Ibid., p. 1321.

often applied for bonds and had to be told: "We are very sorry, but our lists are completely filled and we cannot handle any more."[52]

The strong demand for bonds made foreign lending a very attractive business as the issuing banker knew that selling them at a profit would be easy. In their endeavor to find opportunities for lending, the bankers stretched their concepts of safety, sometimes to a degree strange to behold in retrospect. The following reasoning about loans to German corporations is an illustration. "Of course here when an industrial company borrows, we expect it to have a very beautiful position of liquid capital. I think in Germany in many cases, while the liquid capital was very much less, they had really very substantial amounts of worth that made the loans on the whole very safe."[53]

This argument for the safety of Peruvian loans is another example: ". . . we paid it over to the Government, not in one lump sum as they wished and asked, but $750,000 monthly, on the ground, we said, that they could not economically spend a large amount at once . . . we were instrumental in getting the President to designate a United States Army officer to report upon the public works then being carried on in Peru. We felt that there was construction going on which we ourselves perhaps would not have selected. . . ."[54] How can a loan be deemed safe if the borrower cannot be trusted with the 'lump sum' for which he asks and is, moreover, suspected of using the monthly instalments he receives in undesirable ways?

An atmosphere dangerous to due consideration of risk had arisen. The typical attitude of many bankers resembled that described by Lawrence Dennis with reference to Peru: "When I went down there in 1928, they were contemplating the second loan. I took the very strong position that it was not sound, and I immediately became involved in a long debate, that went on as long as I stayed with the firm, and I was constantly called upon to substantiate my conclusions. . . . They wanted to convince me,

---

[52] Mr. Kahn, ibid., pp. 142 and 394.
[53] George Murnane, Lee, Higginson & Co., ibid., p. 1558.
[54] Mr. Breck, ibid., p. 1287.

as well as to convince themselves, that the loans were sound. . . . They believed it themselves . . . they said that I was pessimistic, and that these things would work themselves out. . . . They took into consideration the facts, but they did nothing effective to correct the evils I pointed out. . . . They made the loans, nevertheless."[55]

The keen competition among bankers described in Section 2 contributed to this carelessness. ". . . if they had not made the loan, someone else would. That was their general reasoning."[56]

Years of reckless lending in a borrowers' market followed years of sober lending in a lenders' market. Decisive for this change was that the bankers, because of the public's confidence they themselves had helped to create, were assured of a market for any loan they floated. The strongest brake on their issuing activity, fear of loss, was eliminated and regard for their reputation remained the sole restraining factor. This again was weakened with many bankers because they themselves erred in the same direction as the public.

Nevertheless, some bankers understood the situation well and, foregoing present profits in order to safeguard their reputation, refrained from making doubtful loans. Their place, however, was quickly taken by others who, sharing the illusions of the public, were ready to lend more or less indiscriminately.

We have seen that the particular economic conditions of the 1920's were responsible for the growing propensity of both bankers and public to make mistakes in foreign lending, and studies by others have shown that some other types of investment were affected similarly. Have periods of this type, major cyclical expansions, generally been characterized by progressive deterioration of new investments? Further investigation of various types of investment in other major expansions in this or in other countries will be re-

---

[55] Ibid., pp. 1599-1601.   [56] Ibid., p. 1601.

quired to determine this. Fluctuations in the volume of investments are generally recognized as a major factor in business cycles; perhaps further investigation will disclose that these changes in volume have typically been supplemented and accentuated by variations in quality.

Appendix Tables

Table 13

Foreign Government Bonds and Domestic Securities Issued in the United States, and Domestic Bond Yields

QUARTER	FOREIGN GOVERN- MENT BOND ISSUES	DOMESTIC ISSUES Common stocks	Bonds	YIELDS ON HIGH- GRADE DOMES- TIC BONDS	FOREIGN GOVERN- MENT BOND ISSUES	DOMESTIC ISSUES Common stocks	Bonds	YIELDS ON HIGH- GRADE DOMES- TIC BONDS
	\multicolumn{3}{c}{Par Value of Flotations in Millions of Dollars}	%	\multicolumn{3}{c}{Par Value of Flotations in Millions of Dollars}	%
	(1)	(2)	(3)	(4)	(5)	(6)	(7)	(8)
	\multicolumn{4}{c}{RAW DATA}	\multicolumn{4}{c}{FOUR QUARTER MOVING AVERAGES*}
1920								
I	64	193	378	5.84				
II	104	209	471	6.22				
III	156	45	450	6.29	114	119	482	6.15
IV	115	93	509	6.13	124	80	561	6.17
1921								
I	98	66	615	6.10	129	63	629	6.12
II	146	23	868	6.12	131	59	697	6.03
III	160	98	599	6.01	153	46	770	5.87
IV	128	7	905	5.65	191	46	823	5.64
1922								
I	258	46	797	5.29	193	54	873	5.38
II	288	43	1,110	5.12	171	64	859	5.18
III	33	139	764	4.96	148	75	853	5.08
IV	81	49	621	5.05	100	86	850	5.06
1923								
I	122	88	1,034	5.10	75	80	786	5.09
II	43	97	854	5.18	78	74	791	5.12
III	75	37	506	5.11	87	88	803	5.12
IV	64	102	918	5.10	105	113	814	5.10
1924								
I	212	145	834	5.09	130	129	897	5.06
II	98	236	1,144	5.04	188	128	937	5.02
III	219	30	880	4.95	219	121	965	4.98
IV	384	100	861	4.94	225	100	1,001	4.94
1925								
I	141	94	1,116	4.94	241	96	1,000	4.91
II	215	114	1,150	4.86	223	124	1,007	4.89
III	230	122	865	4.88	206	151	1,023	4.86
IV	232	228	936	4.85	205	173	1,040	4.83
1926								
I	155	189	1,166	4.79	184	180	1,056	4.79
II	190	189	1,238	4.72	168	161	1,083	4.75
III	91	104	900	4.72	178	147	1,161	4.71
IV	238	97	1,121	4.69	195	146	1,285	4.68

TABLE 13

Table 13 (concluded)

QUARTER	FOREIGN GOVERNMENT BOND ISSUES (1)	DOMESTIC ISSUES Common stocks (2)	Bonds (3)	YIELDS ON HIGH-GRADE DOMESTIC BONDS (4)	FOREIGN GOVERNMENT BOND ISSUES (5)	DOMESTIC ISSUES Common stocks (6)	Bonds (7)	YIELDS ON HIGH-GRADE DOMESTIC BONDS (8)
	Par Value of Flotations in Millions of Dollars			%	*Par Value of Flotations in Millions of Dollars*			%
	RAW DATA				FOUR QUARTER MOVING AVERAGES*			
1927								
I	233	212	1,606	4.65	214	145	1,362	4.64
II	250	153	1,787	4.58	240	150	1,432	4.60
III	179	136	969	4.57	264	142	1,486	4.55
IV	361	99	1,614	4.49	286	177	1,424	4.52
1928								
I	303	147	1,539	4.46	289	232	1,324	4.51
II	355	500	1,364	4.51	249	348	1,212	4.54
III	95	230	590	4.62	188	575	1,088	4.58
IV	122	935	1,097	4.60	124	759	1,002	4.63
1929								
I	54	1,122	1,062	4.66	82	1,014	996	4.68
II	94	1,002	1,157	4.72	68	1,154	983	4.71
III	21	1,763	748	4.79	70	1,001	995	4.73
IV	84	521	833	4.73	105	850	1,063	4.71
1930								
I	109	318	1,421	4.66	136	589	1,104	4.65
II	317	595	1,346	4.59	139	326	1,098	4.58
III	45	83	883	4.47				
IV	89	96	649	4.47				

* Centered by means of a moving average of two items.

COLUMN

1. Foreign government and government guaranteed bonds of a term of 2 years or more, publicly offered in the United States. Adapted from Department of Commerce *Handbook on American Underwriting of Foreign Securities* (1930), pp. 75-132.

2. Compiled by *Commercial and Financial Chronicle*. Quoted from *Survey of Current Business*, Feb. 1938, pp. 14 ff.

3. All long term domestic bonds except federal government. Source same as for column 2.

4. Moody's index of yields on 30 high-grade domestic corporate bonds; *Survey of Current Business*, Nov. 1937, p. 19.

Table 14

Default Status, at the Close of 1937, of Foreign Government Bonds Issued in the United States

Four Quarter Moving Averages, Centered

QUARTER WHEN OFFERED	SAMPLE A[a] ISSUED BY BORROWERS WHO were not IN DEFAULT $ million (1)	were IN DEFAULT $ million (2)	DEFAULT INDEX[c] % (3)	SAMPLE B[b] ISSUED BY BORROWERS WHO were not IN DEFAULT $ million (4)	were IN DEFAULT $ million (5)	DEFAULT INDEX % (6)	PRICE INDEX OF DEFAULTED BONDS (SAMPLE A)[d] % (7)
1920							
III	103	11	9.6	71	10	12.3	55.1
IV	108	16	12.8	80	15	15.7	33.8
1921							
I	109	21	15.9	74	20	21.0	22.6
II	101	30	22.9	65	29	31.0	22.3
III	120	33	21.6	88	32	26.6	21.2
IV	150	40	21.2	103	39	27.5	21.8
1922							
I	146	47	24.2	93	45	32.5	21.5
II	130	41	23.7	86	39	31.1	21.6
III	111	37	24.7	68	34	33.6	23.0
IV	78	23	22.5	51	20	27.9	24.7
1923							
I	66	9	11.9	51	7	11.4	26.6
II	71	7	8.8	53	4	7.3	31.3
III	82	5	6.1	61	2	3.2	41.3
IV	100	5	4.7	77	2	2.9	43.2
1924							
I	123	7	5.2	94	4	4.5	46.4
II	164	24	12.6	131	22	14.5	33.8
III	172	47	21.4	141	47	25.0	33.7
IV	165	60	26.6	131	59	31.2	35.4
1925							
I	169	72	29.8	139	71	33.6	34.2
II	150	74	33.1	125	73	36.6	31.9
III	138	68	33.1	109	67	37.9	29.6
IV	127	78	38.2	93	77	45.3	28.2
1926							
I	98	87	47.0	66	86	56.7	27.7
II	75	93	55.4	46	92	66.4	26.8
III	74	104	58.2	51	102	66.6	25.4
IV	95	100	51.4	72	98	57.7	23.6
1927							
I	117	97	45.2	88	94	51.6	22.9
II	127	113	47.0	92	111	54.7	24.7
III	124	141	53.3	85	140	62.2	26.3
IV	115	171	59.7	85	171	66.7	25.8

TABLE 14

Table 14 (concluded)

QUARTER WHEN OFFERED	SAMPLE A[a] ISSUED BY BORROWERS WHO were not IN DEFAULT $ million (1)	ISSUED BY BORROWERS WHO were IN DEFAULT $ million (2)	DEFAULT INDEX[c] % (3)	SAMPLE B[b] ISSUED BY BORROWERS WHO were not IN DEFAULT $ million (4)	ISSUED BY BORROWERS WHO were IN DEFAULT $ million (5)	DEFAULT INDEX % (6)	PRICE INDEX OF DEFAULTED BONDS (SAMPLE A)[d] % (7)
1928							
I	100	189	65.3	79	189	70.5	24.6
II	84	164	66.1	67	164	71.1	23.1
III	69	118	63.1	54	118	68.7	21.4
IV	47	76	61.7	26	76	74.1	20.2
1929							
I	37	45	55.2	10	45	82.4	19.8
II	38	30	43.7	5	29	85.3	22.2
III	46	24	34.8	3	24	89.8	31.3
IV	60	45	42.7	13	45	77.8	35.9
1930							
I	73	63	46.1	25	62	71.4	35.8
II	78	61	43.6	29	61	67.9	37.0

[a] Includes Canadian bonds. [b] Excludes Canadian bonds.
[c] Column 2 divided by the sum of columns 1 and 2.
[d] Average price of defaulted bonds in Sample A at the close of 1937.

Table 15

Default Index Based on Number of Foreign Government Bonds Issued in the United States, 1920-1930

	SAMPLE A			SAMPLE B		
	ISSUED BY BORROWERS			ISSUED BY BORROWERS		
YEAR WHEN OF- FERED	WHO *were not* IN DE- FAULT*	WHO *were* IN DE- FAULT*	DEFAULT INDEX	WHO *were not* IN DE- FAULT*	WHO *were* IN DE- FAULT*	DEFAULT INDEX
	(number of issues)		%	(number of issues)		%
	(1)	(2)	(3)	(4)	(5)	(6)
1920	59	7	11	16	2	11
1921	56	17	23	10	12	55
1922	57	24	30	22	20	48
1923	25	5	17	13	2	13
1924	58	11	16	25	10	29
1925	38	37	49	19	35	65
1926	34	55	62	15	53	78
1927	68	51	43	28	49	64
1928	30	63	68	18	62	78
1929	29	14	33	2	13	87
1930	46	13	22	10	13	56

See notes to Table 14.
* At the close of 1937.

Table 16
Average Size of Issue, 'Sound' and 'Unsound' Foreign Government Bonds Issued in the United States

YEARS WHEN OF- FERED	'SOUND' ISSUES Value ($ mil.) (1)	Num- ber (2)	Aver- age size ($ mil.) (3)	'UNSOUND' ISSUES Value ($ mil.) (4)	Num- ber (5)	Aver- age size ($ mil.) (6)	INDEX (col. 3 ÷ col. 6) (7)
			SAMPLE A[a]				
1920-25	2,596.11	280	9.27	607.18	74	8.21	112.9
1925-30	1,884.35	220	8.57	1,961.17	223	8.79	97.5
			SAMPLE B[b]				
1920-25	1,892.61	97	19.51	570.35	54	10.56	184.8
1925-30	1,150.43	81	14.20	1,944.82	217	8.96	158.5

I quarter 1920 to II quarter 1925 inclusive and III quarter 1925 to IV quarter 1930 inclusive.

[a] Includes Canadian issues.   [b] Excludes Canadian issues.

Table 17

Default Status of Foreign Government Bonds Issued in the United States by Geographic Areas

YEAR WHEN OF-FERED	'SOUND' ISSUES					'UNSOUND' ISSUES			TOTAL
	West and No. Europe	East and Central Europe	Far East	Latin America	Canada	East and Central Europe	Latin America	Canada	
	MILLIONS OF DOLLARS								
1920	276	0	0	0	136	23	0	4	439
1921	205	0	15	50	120	0	137	4	532
1922	142	22	111	54	180	19	125	7	660
1923	56	25	71	55	75	0	8	15	304
1924	393	12	147	78	127	132	22	1	912
1925	261	32	75	75	102	210	58	5	818
1926	86	9	20	43	112	147	249	7	673
1927	115	33	113	93	161	222	230	6	973
1928	154	0	76	27	65	232	318	3	875
1929	4	0	0	0	156	27	65	1	253
1920-24	1,072	59	344	237	638	174	292	31	2,847
1925-29	620	74	284	238	596	838	920	22	3,592
	PERCENTAGES								
1920	62.9	0.0	0.0	0.0	31.0	5.3	0.0	0.8	100
1921	38.6	0.0	2.9	9.4	22.5	0.0	25.8	0.8	100
1922	21.5	3.3	16.8	8.2	27.2	2.9	19.0	1.1	100
1923	18.5	8.2	23.2	18.0	24.6	0.0	2.6	4.9	100
1924	43.1	1.3	16.1	8.6	13.9	14.4	2.4	0.2	100
1925	31.9	3.9	9.2	9.1	12.4	25.7	7.1	0.7	100
1926	12.8	1.3	2.9	6.4	16.7	21.8	37.0	1.1	100
1927	11.9	3.4	11.6	9.6	16.5	22.8	23.6	0.6	100
1928	17.6	0.0	8.7	3.1	7.5	26.5	36.3	0.3	100
1929	1.4	0.0	0.0	0.2	61.8	10.6	25.7	0.3	100
1920-24	37.7	2.0	12.1	8.3	22.4	6.1	10.3	1.1	100
1925-29	17.3	2.0	7.9	6.6	16.6	23.4	25.6	0.6	100

See Tables 13 and 14, notes.

Table 18

Risk Premiums on Foreign Government Bonds Issued in the United States

Four Quarter Moving Averages, Centered

Quarter when Offered	Risk Premium[a] (points)	Default Index A Adjusted[b] (%)	Quarter when Offered	Risk Premium[a] (points)	Default Index A Adjusted[b] (%)
1920			1926		
III	2.51	4.9	I	2.26	47.1
IV	2.56	10.8	II	2.32	55.4
1921			III	2.27	58.3
I	2.38	15.9	IV	2.22	51.4
II	2.25	22.8	1927		
III	2.20	21.4	I	2.12	45.2
IV	2.01	20.8	II	2.03	47.0
1922			III	2.00	53.4
I	1.91	23.7	IV	1.99	59.8
II	1.87	23.0	1928		
III	1.73	24.2	I	2.00	65.3
IV	1.62	22.1	II	2.00	66.0
1923			III	1.91	63.1
I	1.55	11.6	IV	1.82	61.7
II	1.45	7.7	1929		
III	1.61	3.9	I	1.71	55.2
IV	1.71	2.9	II	1.47	43.8
1924			III	1.26	34.8
I	1.71	3.8	IV	1.43	42.7
II	1.94	12.1	1930		
III	2.13	21.4	I	1.55	46.1
IV	2.18	26.6	II	1.51	43.8
1925					
I	2.18	29.9			
II	2.21	33.1			
III	2.17	33.1			
IV	2.13	38.2			

[a] Weighted averages of excess of yield on new foreign government bonds over yield on highest grade domestic bonds of similar term to maturity (Durand's 'basic yields').

[b] Default index A (see Table 15) adjusted by exclusion of bond issues whose risk premium could not be ascertained.

Table 19

Uncorrected Default Index of Foreign Government Bonds Issued in the United States

QUARTER WHEN OFFERED	UNCORRECTED DEFAULT INDEX A[a]	B[b]	QUARTER WHEN OFFERED	UNCORRECTED DEFAULT INDEX A[a]	B[b]
1920			1926		
III	6.16	8.62	I	43.37	52.22
IV	7.00	9.01	II	50.65	60.67
			III	53.34	60.90
1921			IV	46.94	52.55
I	10.18	13.84			
II	15.33	21.09	1927		
III	15.38	19.04	I	40.97	46.68
IV	16.40	21.48	II	44.53	51.80
			III	52.17	60.89
1922			IV	59.03	65.95
I	18.07	24.36			
II	17.83	23.35	1928		
III	19.39	26.30	I	65.14	70.34
IV	17.47	21.43	II	65.55	70.59
			III	61.74	67.18
1923			IV	59.57	71.49
I	9.49	8.71			
II	6.67	6.17	1929		
III	3.77	3.18	I	51.94	77.45
IV	2.43	2.45	II	41.71	81.20
			III	34.72	89.51
1924			IV	42.70	77.61
I	2.89	3.43			
II	10.84	13.05	1930		
III	19.82	23.08	I	46.13	71.42
IV	25.06	29.31	II	43.62	67.88
1925					
I	28.48	32.09			
II	31.11	34.42			
III	30.49	34.87			
IV	35.27	41.76			

All repaid issues are classified as sound issues. See Chapter 2, Section 2.

[a] Includes Canadian bonds.   [b] Excludes Canadian bonds.

INDEX

Angell, James W., 15-6, 71-2
Argentina, 16-7, 31, 43; *see also* Latin America
default index, 50-1
Australia, 16-7, 51; *see also* Far East
Austria, 16-7, 33, 51; *see also* Eastern Europe

Balance of payments, relation to foreign bond cycles, 13-5
Bank of England, control of lending by, 19
Banking houses, 54-8, 63-85
  cautiousness of, 64-5
  competition for foreign loans by, 65-7, 85
  default indexes for individual, 55-8
  estimates of risk by, 73-8
  importance of their reputation to, 78-80
  investigation of borrowers by, 73-5
  issuing defined, 54
  public's reliance on, 64, 79, 81-2
Basic yields, definition, 59; *see also* Risk; Risk premium
Belgium, 43, 51, 69; *see also* Western Europe
Bloomfield, Arthur I., 14, 20
Bolivia, 29-30, 43; *see also* Latin America
Bond prices; *see* Bonds, foreign government
Bondholders, foreign; *see* Foreign bondholders
Bonds, domestic
  cyclical pattern of issues, 22-3
  default status, 45-6
  inverse relation of issues to business cycles, 20-3
  par value of flotations, 88-9
  yields, 88-9
Bonds, foreign, 1-7; *see also* Bonds, foreign government; Capital issues
Bonds, foreign government
  amounts floated, 8-9, 19, 28, 52, 55, 57, 88-9, 93
  amount held by investors, average, 81
  character of investors, 80-1
  cycles in issues compared with American business cycles, 11-3, 16-8, 20-8
  domestic bond issues, 20-3
  domestic common stock issues, 24-7
  foreign business cycles, 15-20
  interest rate, 23-4
  major business cycle, 12-3
  default; *see* Default; Default index
  demand for by public, 80-3
  examination before granting, 73-8
  geographic distribution of borrowers, 50-3
  history, 8-9
  investors' motives for buying, 81-2
  losses on, 2
  negotiation of issues, 63-8
  number of issues, 92
  par value of flotations; *see* amounts floated
  post-war status, 43-4
  prices of defaulted, 41-3
  procedure of floating, 54n
  propaganda for, 64
  quality; *see* Quality
  risk premium on, 59-62, 70, 94
  safety provisions, 74-5
  size of issue, average, 92
  sound and unsound issues, 31-2; *see also* Default; Default index
  terms, 10
  yields; *see* Yields
Brazil, 16-7, 29-30, 42; *see also* Latin America
Breck, Henry C., 64, 83-4
Brown, William Adams, Jr., 15, 20, 45
Buchanan, Norman S., 1, 2, 7
Bulgaria, 30, 51; *see also* Eastern Europe
Burns, Arthur F., 5, 16, 22
Business cycles; *see* Bonds, domestic; Bonds, foreign government; Common stock issues; Debtor countries; Default index

Canada, 8, 15, 30-1, 44, 50, 54, 70, 72; *see also* Default index
government bonds floated in U. S. amount, 52

97

Canada (*concl.*)
　default index, 51
　relation to total issues, 10, 52
　sound and unsound issues, 53, 93
Capital exports, cyclical movements, 13-6
Capital issues, U. S. total foreign, amount and number, 8-9
Central Europe, 51
Chase, Harris, Forbes Corporation, 74
Chase National Bank, 75
Chile, 29-30, 80-1; *see also* Latin America
China, 29
Clark, J. M., 13
Colombia, 30, 65, 67; *see also* Latin America
Commerce, U. S. Department of, 8, 9, 10, 19, 27, 28, 62, 74, 89
Commercial and Financial Chronicle, 89
Common stock issues
　cycles in domestic, and in foreign government bonds, 24-8
　domestic, par value, 88-9
　foreign, in U. S., 10, 28
Corliss, James C., 65
Corporate foreign issues, 9
Costa Rica, 30; *see also* Latin America
Country banks, competition for foreign loans by, 83
Cuba, 29-31, 43, 50-1, 75; *see also* Latin America
　default index, 51
Czechoslovakia, 31, 50-1; *see also* Eastern Europe

Danzig, 51; *see also* Eastern Europe
Dawes loan, year of default, 30, 58
Dawes Plan, 26
Debtor countries
　cycles in their business and in U. S. foreign bond issues, 15-8
　geographic location of related to loan quality, 50-3
Default, 29-49; *see also* Banking houses; Bonds, domestic; Default index; Risk premium
　absence of in twenties, 29, 71
　definition, 31-7, 44
　degree; *see* partial
　factors leading to, 2-3, 6-7, 29-30, 63-85
　history, 29-31

　partial, 30-1, 34, 40-4, 50-1; *see also* Argentina; Canada; Cuba; Czechoslovakia; Dominican Republic; Guatemala; Panama
　relation to amount of bonds, 2
　relation to geographic location of debtor country, 50-3
Default index, 29-49
　based on banking houses initiating loans, 54-7
　based on borrowers' geographic location, 50-2
　based on number of issues, 39-40
　based on post-war status of bonds, 43-4
　Canadian loans excluded from, 37, 39-40, 90-1, 92, 95
　cyclical fluctuations, 37-40
　method of computation, 33-7
　risk premium compared with, 60-2, 94
Denmark, 44; *see also* Western Europe
Dennis, Lawrence, 77, 84
Deterioration; *see* Quality
District of Columbia, 81
Domestic bonds; *see* Bonds, domestic
Dominican Republic, 43; *see also* Latin America
Durand, David, 59-60, 94

Eastern Europe, 51-3, 68-9, 93; *see also* individual countries
Edwards, George W., 4, 45-6, 54
El Salvador, 30; *see also* Latin America
England; *see* Great Britain
Estonia, 51; *see also* Eastern Europe
Europe, 10, 16, 30, 33, 50-3, 66; *see also* Eastern Europe; Western Europe; individual countries
Exchange control, 29
Export surplus, relation to business cycles, 13

Far East, 10, 51-3, 72, 93; *see also* individual countries
Finland, 51; *see also* Western Europe
Flotations; *see* Banking houses; Bonds, domestic; Bonds, foreign government; Capital issues; Common stock issues

Foreclosure rates, 48
Foreign bondholders, number of, 81
Foreign Bondholders' Protective Council, 31, 33, 80-1
Foreign bonds; *see* Bonds, foreign government
Foreign capital issues; *see* Capital issues
Foreign government bonds; *see* Bonds, foreign government
Foreign lending, 3-7, 45, 71-2; *see also* Bonds, foreign government; Capital issues; Common stock issues; World War I
Foreign loans; *see* Bonds, foreign government; Capital issues; Common stock issues
Foreign trade, U. S., relation to capital exports, 14-5
France, 8, 16-7, 26, 43, 51, 69; *see also* Western Europe

Germany, 16-7, 26, 29-30, 41-2, 51, 68-9, 84; *see also* Eastern Europe
Gilbert, S. Parker, 74, 77
Gold clause, 33
Granberry, E. C., 74, 79
Great Britain, 8, 9, 15, 51, 74; *see also* Western Europe
 foreign lending compared with American, 18-20
 foreign government securities issued, 19
Greece, 30, 51; *see also* Eastern Europe
Guatemala, 43; *see also* Latin America

Haberler, Gottfried, 5
Handbook, 8, 9, 19, 27-8, 62
Hearings; *see* U. S. Senate
Holland; *see* Netherlands
Hungary, 30, 51, 64; *see also* Eastern Europe

Institute of International Finance, 31
Interest rates, related to foreign bond issues, 23-4
Investors in foreign government bonds, 80-2
Ireland, 51; *see also* Western Europe

Issuing bank; *see* Banking houses
Italy, 16-7, 51; *see also* Western Europe

Japan, 51; *see also* Far East
Johnson, Senator Hiram W., 65
Jones, Grosvenor M., 67-8

Kahn, Otto H., 64, 67, 78-9, 84
Kimber Co., A. W., 31
Kuhn, Loeb & Co., 64, 68, 74

Lamont, Thomas W., 64, 66, 74, 77-8
Lary, Hal B., 1, 3, 20, 23, 24
Latin America, 10, 30, 42-3, 51-3, 66-9, 72, 93; *see also* individual countries
Lee, Higginson & Co., 84
Lewis, Cleona, 2, 3
Lisman & Co., F. J., 66
Lisman, Frederick J., 65-6, 83
Loan quality, index of; *see* Default index
Loans, foreign; *see* Bonds, foreign government
Lutz, Friedrich A., 1

Madden, J. T., 2, 3, 30, 34, 61, 78
Midland Bank, 19
Mitchell, Charles E., 81
Mitchell, Wesley C., 5, 7, 12, 16, 18, 22
Moody's, 23, 60, 89; *see also* Yields
Morgan & Co., J. P., 64, 68
Morrow, Dwight W., 80
Mortgage loans, urban, 47-9
 foreclosure rates, 48
Moving averages, 11
Murnane, George, 84

Nadler, Marcus, 2, 3, 30, 34, 61, 78
National City Bank, 81n
Netherlands, 16-7, 51, 74; *see also* Western Europe
Netherlands Indies, 51; *see also* Far East
Northern Europe, 51
Norway, 43, 64, 69; *see also* Western Europe
Nurkse, Ragnar, 1, 3

Palestine, 51; *see also* Far East
Panama, 30-1, 50-1; *see also* Latin America
  default index, 51
Peru, 29-30, 43, 66-7, 76-7, 84; *see also* Latin America
Poland, 30, 51; *see also* Eastern Europe
Prices; *see* Bonds, foreign government
Private foreign capital issues, 9

Quality of domestic bonds, 45-6
Quality of foreign government bonds
  decline interpreted, 63-85
  ex ante estimates of, 59-62
  relation of to time of issue, 4, 6, 7, 31-2, 37-40, 45
    and geographic location of borrower, 50-3
    and initiating banking house, 54-8
Quality of mortgages, 46-9

Risk; *see also* Risk premium
  bankers' estimates of, 58, 73-80, 83-5
  importance of to bankers, 78-80
  investors' attitude to, 69-71, 81-2
Risk premium, 59-62
  and analysis of change, 70
  comparison with default index, 61, 94
  definition, 59
Royal Institute of International Affairs, 29
Rumania, 30, 51; *see also* Eastern Europe
Rushmore, Bisbee & Stern, 75

Salter, Sir Arthur, 2, 6, 56
Saulnier, R. J., 4, 46, 47, 48
Sauvain, Harry, 2, 3, 30, 34, 61, 78
Scandinavia, 51; *see also* Western Europe
Schacht, Hjalmar, 74
Schumpeter, J. A., 5
Securities and Exchange Commission, 81
Security issues; *see* Bonds, domestic; Bonds, foreign government; Capital issues; Common stock issues

Seligman & Co., J. & W., 64, 65, 76-7
Sound and unsound issues; *see* Bonds, foreign government
Speyer & Co., 64
Speyer, James, 64, 79
Spread, 64-5, 66-7
Stocks; *see* Common stock issues
Strauss, Frederick, 65, 67
Sudetenland, 33
Switzerland, 51; *see also* Western Europe

Territories and possessions, 10
Thorp, W. L., 16
Townsend, Oliver C., 66
Trade balance; *see* Balance of payments
Transfer
  problem of, 3, 6-7
  prohibition by defaulting government, 30

Underwriting syndicate, 54
United Kingdom; *see* Great Britain
United Nations, 3
U. S. Senate
  Committee on Banking and Currency, 75
  Committee on Finance, Hearings before, 63-85
Uruguay, 30; *see also* Latin America

Warnings against overborrowing, 77
Western Europe, 51-3, 93; *see also* individual countries
White, Weld & Co., 31
Williams, A. M., 75
Winkler, Max, 45, 66, 77
World War I, influence on foreign lending, 8, 69

Yields, 24, 27, 59-62, 65, 70, 88-9; *see also* Basic yields
Young, Ralph A., 8, 9
Young loan, year of default, 30, 58
Young Plan, 27
Yugoslavia, 30; *see also* Eastern Europe